THE BEGINNER'S GUIDE
TO THE
FINANCIAL UNIVERSE

D1571616

Also by Christeen Skinner

The Financial Universe
Exploring the Financial Universe

THE BEGINNER'S GUIDE TO THE FINANCIAL UNIVERSE

*An Introduction to the Role of
the Sun, Moon, and Planets
in Financial Markets*

Christeen H. Skinner

Ibis Press
Lake Worth, Florida

Published in 2017 by Ibis Press
A division of Nicolas-Hays, Inc.
P. O. Box 540206
Lake Worth, FL 33454-0206
www.ibispress.net

Distributed to the trade by
Red Wheel/Weiser, LLC
65 Parker St. • Ste. 7
Newburyport, MA 01950
www.redwheelweiser.com

Library of Congress Cataloging-in-Publication Data
Available Upon Request

ISBN 978-0-89254-224-6
Ebook: ISBN 978-0-89254-640-4

Book design and production by Studio 31
www.studio31.com

Cover image
EPA/ANSA/Alessandro di Meo

[MV]
Printed in the United States of America

CONTENTS

Chart of Astrological Glyphs

These glyphs are shown throughout the Optuma charts that illustrate this book

	SIGNS		PLANETS
Glyph	**Name**	**Gyph**	**Name**
♈	Aries	☽	Moon
♉	Taurus	☉	Sun
♊	Gemini	☿	Mercury
♋	Cancer	♀	Venus
♌	Leo	♂	Mars
♍	Virgo	♃	Jupiter
♎	Libra	♄	Saturn
♏	Scorpio	♅	Uranus
♐	Sagittarius	♆	Neptune
♑	Capricorn	♇	Pluto
♒	Aquarius		
♓	Pisces		

	ASTEROIDS		ASSORTED
Glyph	**Name**	**Glyphs**	**Name**
⚷	Chiron	☊	North Node
⚶	Vesta	☋	South Node
⚴	Pallas	Asc.	Ascendant
⚵	Juno	Mc	Midheaven
⚳	Ceres	⊕	Part of Fortune

ASPECTS

Glyph	**Name**	**Angle**
☌	Conjunction	0°
∨	Semi-sextile	30°
∠	Semi Square	45°
⚹	Sextile	60°
Q	Quintile	72°
□	Square	90°
△	Trine	120°
⚼	Sesquiquadrate	135°
—	Quincunx	150°
☍	Opposition	180°
‖	Parallel	
⚵	Contra-Parallel	

Preface

THE CONTENTS OF THIS BOOK WILL NOT teach you how to trade. To be a successful trader requires levels of skill, talent, and training that this book in no way attempts to provide.

Nor does the information contained herein provide the would-be trader with any inside track to guaranteed profit.

So why then write this book?

The easy, short, and truthful answer is that students and clients have asked for it.

I have worked with traders now for over 30 years and have come to the conclusion that the use of planetary cycles coupled with an understanding of the psychology behind trading can offer traders a leading edge in their work.

It has been my experience that financial astrology can be that perfect extra tool in the trader's toolbox: delivering a degree of mastery over time and, occasionally, of price.

As will be seen, the employment of planetary cycles is not easy: there are many factors to be taken into consideration.

Thus, this book is the BEGINNER'S Guide—which I hope will be followed by an Intermediate Guide at a later date.

Astrologers should note, that some of the ideas and even facts suggested in this work will contradict traditional thinking. It took me some time to accept that although there were many instances when markets responded to traditional aspects as might be expected, the really big stories occurred using angles or time measurement not generally practiced by the average astrologer.

I should perhaps have begun this work many years ago and even now wonder if it is too soon to be sharing the results of my preliminary research (20 years so far and counting). However, I am reminded constantly by both students and clients, of how little is available in this field and how important it is to help expand the research and the conversation.

I have also wrestled with the dilemma of exactly where to start. Do I begin with the intricacies of certain planet cycles—all with significant events in the market—and then try to decode these? Or do I examine successful (and poor) trades to decode the planetary alignments involved?

As this work is intended even for readers with little understanding of the planets and their traditional astrological meanings, I have included short essays about each planet's significance in financial astrology en route to incorporating some key planetary pairs. I use the term "planet" loosely as there is a chapter on the Sun, others on the Moon, and the Lunar Nodes. I also share my thoughts on the importance of exact timing and the key angles operating at a selected time and place (i.e., the rising and culminating degrees, or Ascendant [ASC] and Midheaven [MC] of a given horoscope).

Occasionally I do offer possible trading strategies which, when combined with technical analysis or guidance from someone well versed in trading, might be considered.

Back-testing—or reverse engineering—of the ideas presented should be viewed as a mandatory part of your personal curriculum. Whereas within this book examples cover the Standard and Poor Index (SPX), the Dow Jones Index (DJI), and Euro-US dollar trading (EURUSD), there are many more trading platforms that have not been given adequate research.

Through this work I hope to enthuse those teased by the concept of links between movements in our solar system and activity in the financial markets.

And I welcome feedback.

Introduction

Wʜᴀᴛ ᴋɪɴᴅ ᴏғ ʙᴇɢɪɴɴᴇʀ ᴀʀᴇ ʏᴏᴜ? Are you a trader with no knowledge of astrology or an astrologer with little knowledge of the markets?

If you are the former, then you will need to learn a little of the language or alphabet of astrology. A glossary explaining terms such as "ecliptic" and "declination" is given at the back of the book, while a guide to the symbols (glyphs) used for the twelve signs of the zodiac, the planets, and the angles or aspects made by them is offered following this introduction.

One of the best definitions of astrology was written by Priscilla Costello, author of *The Weiser Concise Guide to Practical Astrology*. She states that:

> Astrology is the calculation and meaningful interpretation of the positions and motions of the heavenly bodies and their correlation with human experience.

Financial astrology attempts to correlate specific patterns made by the planets as they wander through the heavens with definite movements in the markets. Research offers compelling results as shown in my book *Exploring the Financial Universe*. As particular planets pass through certain areas of the sky, turbulence is common. Market tops and losses have coincided with the formation of particular angles (aspects) between planets.

It would certainly be helpful to read through *The Weiser Concise Guide to Practical Astrology* while studying this Beginner's Guide. Understanding the nature of each sign and, indeed, each planet and aspect will prove invaluable as your studies take you toward forecasting movements in the markets.

THE SIGNS

The twelve signs used here form the Tropical Zodiac. The signs of the zodiac we will be discussing are not the same as the constellations or groups of stars in the heavens. True, there are constellations with the same names. Unlike the constellations however, the signs of the tropical zodiac are of equal length.

Each sign of this tropical zodiac relates to a particular type of human experience: for example, the first sign, Aries, is thought of as energetic, hot, volatile, aggressive, action-packed, promising, brave, cutting-edge, impulsive, and risk-taking. Similar lists of keywords can be created for each sign. What is recognized by financial astrologers is that the passage of the Sun, Moon or planet through each sign coincides with trading behavior reminiscent of these keywords.

THE PLANETS

The planets listed and used in this work are those which can be seen either by the naked eye or through one of NASA's telescopes. Their orbits have been calculated and their positions for many, many years ahead can be listed in tables known as ephemerides.

Just as the signs are associated with certain characteristics, so too are the planets. You will already be familiar with many of these. The terms "mercurial" comes from Mercury itself, while "saturnine" comes from Saturn, and "jovial" from Jupiter. You may be surprised by how much you already know.

Putting signs and planets together can be fun. For example, suppose that Saturn is moving through Aries. Saturnine Saturn would surely put the brake on Aries risk-taking—or at least demand that those taking risks accept the responsibility if it all goes wrong!

ASPECTS

The angles formed between planets are commonly referred to as aspects. In traditional astrology, some were thought of as "bad" and some "good." Financial astrology differs greatly from natal astrology in that all angles are considered. If, for example, we were to find that a price moved whenever two planets are, say, 33 degrees apart, then full focus would be given to that particular rhythm. More regular astrology focuses on angles or aspects created by the division of the circle by 2, 3, 4, 5, 6, 12, 15 or 24. The financial astrologer is not limited in this way. However, in this Beginner's Guide, focus is given to these basic aspects.

HOROSCOPE

Even if you are new to astrology, you may have seen a horoscope: in the West, usually a circle divided into twelve sectors. The planets are positioned within this circle with the signs usually placed on the outer rim.

It is not necessary to be able to read one of these charts to enter the world of financial astrology.

That said, it is worth noting that each of these charts can be divided into quadrants. The quadrants are marked by the "Ascendant" and its opposite, the "Descendant" (the horizontal axis of the horoscope) and the "MC" and "IC" (respectively the top and bottom of the horoscope providing a vertical axis).

Each quadrant has its own unique starting position, which is determined by the exact time and place for which the specific chart is cast.

Not every financial astrologer casts precise horoscopes. Many show a preference for the aspects, or relationships, made by the planets to each other.

HOUSES

Those new to astrology will surely be unfamiliar with the term "houses." The houses of a horoscope—generally twelve in number—may be calculated in many (over 30!) different ways. These houses may be thought of as demarcations. They do have value in financial astrology but are not explored in this beginner's work.

TECHNICAL CHARTS

Many charts are offered in this book. Each bar shows the low and high price on a given day. Day charts are used throughout. Though many traders study weekly and monthly charts, astrology offers the possibility of fine-tuning to select specific dates when marked action (usually change of direction) is likely.

AND FINALLY

Whatever kind of "beginner" you are, it is hoped that this work offers something for you. It would be very disappointing indeed if readers felt daunted or confused. This book is intended to enthuse and encourage further study. Should you have further questions, then please do visit www.financialuniverse.co.uk.

—Christeen Skinner
December 2016

Chapter 1

Who, Why, and When?

THIS BEGINNERS GUIDE TO FINANCIAL ASTROLOGY must start with:

Who?, Why?, When?
The key question is, of course, How?

This chapter aims to answer the first three questions The remainder of the book is an attempt to show "How" planetary cycles and market behavior are interlinked.

Who?

There is an often used quote attributed to J. P. Morgan that "millionaires don't use astrology, but billionaires do." I don't know whether his saying that is myth or fact. What I do know is that there are some individuals—and, indeed, certain generations—more willing to give credence to the correlation between planetary cycles and market trends than others.

In particular, my observation is that many of today's traders are intrigued, fascinated, and curious to know more—particularly those people who were born in the mid-1960s under rare planetary configurations. Members of this group are not fazed by being thought of as "outliers" and are content to make use of any system as long as it works. They might analyze levels of Swiss rainfall, rings on trees, or space weather conditions in their quest to find pattern and correlation with price fluctuations; blending the results with their understanding of market behavior (usually in the form of technical analysis). Their ongoing quest to decode the markets usually means they don't rule out any system. Curiosity about the possible link between "stars and markets" is not, of course, confined to those of this generation (nor are they ALL interested). The one fact that applies to all these people though is that they are only interested in what works—for them.

In that last sentence the keywords are "what works" and "for them." Fact is that one person's "system" may not work for someone else. Much depends on the type of trader and the markets in which they work.

The answer then to the "Who" part of our question is—anyone. I can only speak from my own experience, but the further up the chain of command the trader is within a company, the more likely it is that he or she will be at least receptive to the use of planetary cycles in forecasting—if not actively using this information already. Yes, this does include the Chairmen of banks, the CEOs of companies, hedge fund managers, and financial advisors.

Journalists would love it if I were to "name names" and yes, for sceptics this would surely give momentary pleasure. Yet this is of no real value to anyone: particularly as I cannot think of one client, investor, colleague, or friend who has traded ONLY using astro-information—it is simply a *factor* in their risk assessment and calculations. The "truth" as to how the information is put to use is generally a disappointment to journalists seeking a good story.

It has been my experience that those who want to make full use of financial astrology also have an interest in their own chart. Some will not trade during periods when they feel they are under negative influences. When we have worked together to analyze past and poor decision-making, we have found this to correlate to the effect of planetary transits that could have been signalled well in advance. Now alert to these trends, some traders I know will simply not countenance trading if a variation on the planetary pictures of those earlier times are set to repeat.

I cannot quantify the number of traders using astro-techniques and don't know of any research done in this area. I should say that I would also be slightly suspicious of the results if a survey of City traders using financial astrology were to be carried out (even if done anonymously). Part of the reason is that traders don't always know they are making use of astrology, per se. Though many will take account of New and Full Moons and, certainly in the City of London, the times of high and low tides (which often coincide with increased economic activity), they might not consider themselves to be using astrological techniques or see their behavior as being linked to cycles at work within our solar system.

Though younger traders (especially those born since the mid-1960s) have few qualms about discussing the role of the planets and trading, I have noted some reticence among older generations. Yet going back about 20 years or more, I recall too that there were many who did not wish it to be known that they were making use of astrology—even as they walked about with worn copies of ephemerides in their jacket pockets. These traders might well deny their interest if subjected to a survey. I remember one particular lunch time conversation with a highly respected economist and trader whose copy of the ephemeris for that year had dates highlighted and copious notes made in the margins. While he might well have denied his interest to some people, he was quite open in our conversation. Indeed, I was amazed to learn the thoroughness of his understanding and the sophisticated knowledge of harmonics that he put to good use.

Why?

So why do some people make use of planetary cycles? The short answer is that some traders recall instances where they can show that it gave them significant advantage. These traders have profited by making use of a tool which has been described to me as a "master timer." Others have heard such success stories and are anxious to explore any tool that may actually work.

Note that it is generally true of individuals who make use of astro-information—not companies. It's hard to imagine that, in the West anyway, a board meeting decision would be made to seek the opinion of an astrologer. However, the same is not true in many other parts of the world. In India particularly, there is general acceptance of a link between patterns formed by the planets in the solar system and general behavior. Meetings may take place at times suggested by an astrologer and contracts signed at what have been deemed to be auspicious times.

Upon occasion I have been asked by a UK company to explain why a certain time and date have been chosen for such an event. Presumably my clients worry that they might be at a disadvantage and want to be prepared, celestially speaking, for what may or may not ensue. The fact that this request has been made repeatedly suggests to me that my astrology-based explanations are decreed useful by company executives.

This book is targeted mainly at Western readers. While I have been invited into board meetings of UK companies, such instances have been few and far between. I have also always been aware of the scepticism of some of those seated around the table. My experience is that attempting to work with seasoned sceptics is more likely to lead to hostility than to good working relationships! On the few occasions where there is good rapport, on the other hand, our partnerships have lasted over a quarter of a century.

Canny investors, chief executives, financial advisers, and the like place great store in risk assessment. They do not bother with systems that do not work. Generally, they are prepared to accept that detailed analysis and reports take time to prepare. My experience has been that when I am unsure as to what any particular planetary configurations might bring—and where I'm able to identify a similar celestial pattern from the past—these individuals will gladly make access to archives possible so that a potential trend can be identified.

Those prepared to countenance a potential link between the planets and human behavior are generally receptive to the idea that cosmic patterns could be mirrored in market activity.

Though distressed when I've been wrong, or been wide of the mark, clients have been quick to point out that my reading of configurations does not need to be right 100% of the time. Half a dozen good astrological tips can be sufficient.

As important as forecasting likely daily trends is, the long-term view is also important. Clients value discussions about long-term trends and one refers to me as a "futurologist." That title is more deserved by the NASA scientists and computer software developers whose work permits me to know where the planets will be decades and even centuries into the future. By constantly referring back to similar planetary patterns in the past, and reviewing the history of those earlier periods, it is possible to offer ideas as to what the future may hold.

Serious investors and traders are understandably ruthless in the way in which they work. An ongoing relationship demands good results. These can never be 100%. The answer then as to why investors, traders, hedge fund managers, and financial advisers turn to financial astrology is that they know of instances where it has proven successful. I have little doubt that clients would stop working with me if our success rates were to fall. As it stands—and with the quality of work being produced by the growing number of financial astrologers working across the world continually improving—it seems more likely that the client work-load will increase.

In the late 1980s—and with a rare planetary configuration building—a colleague made the then-astounding forecast that markets would fall substantially in October of 1987. When that forecast proved sound, his client base expanded. I got involved with city traders around this time. In early 1989, while examining a rare planetary configuration due to take place later that year, I offered the opinion that an economic earthquake from the East was likely. Timing suggested that this would take place later at night UK time. I came to the erroneous conclusion that since Asian markets would be just opening for business, any decline would be reaction to events taking place in that part of the world. In fact, the Berlin Wall fell! The forecast was loosely correct.

As I had been precise about the timing of this particular economic movement, traders then pushed me for daily forecasts. This was not an area in which, at that time, I had either the technical ability or expertise. Two traders effectively mentored me during this period. We had regular calls just after 7 a.m. each day, during which I made suggestions as to how I thought markets world react to the lunar and planetary patterns of the day. Until both retired, we enjoyed a highly successful partnership working on the probable Financial Times Stock Exchange (FTSE) levels for the day and, in particular, gold trading.

I was not alone among the growing number of astrologers making political, social and economic forecasts at the turn of the millennium. Much had been made of the possibility of the so-called millennium Y2K bug causing havoc across the world. I met with several traders and investors through 1998 and 1999 who were fearful of the potential difficulties. The planetary pictures for the close of the 20th century and opening of the 21st did not suggest the calamity that they believed possible.

My far greater concern was that in the weeks ahead of the Jupiter-Saturn alignment that would take place at the end of May 2000, some extremely tense configurations would take place, and might well coincide with market drama. What is now termed "the dot.com crash" was exactly on planetary cue. Looking beyond 2000—and like many other astrologers—I was concerned that Pluto's arrival in Capricorn would coincide with the collapse of banking structures and potentially, the bankruptcy of some countries. I wrote about this in my book, *The Financial Universe* published in 2004.

The answer to the "Why?" question then is that knowledge of planetary pictures has proven helpful and, at times, resulted in profit.

When?

Understandably, following on from these earlier forecasts, my work-load expanded. This suggested to me not only that potential clients were intrigued to know more, but that when the markets are in disarray—and when decline arrives as an apparent surprise to other forecasters—the use of astrological techniques becomes a topic of compelling interest.

In preparing this book and reviewing the last twenty years, I note that years of greatest interest in my work have coincided with major planetary configurations (a hardly surprising correlation to an astrologer!). Traders might not know that Jupiter will be at right-angle to Saturn for example, but they do sense turning points. When following "gut instinct," such tuned-in people will seek affirmation that "something is happening."

It is also true that inquiries from traders experiencing loss or crisis are more common than those who have "general interest." Most people tend to seek out planetary assistance when they surmise that no other system is working for them.

Working with a new trading client is more challenging. Often they may be raw from negative experience. It might even be that they seek quick and fast solutions to get them out of trouble. This is rarely possible: it is imperative to first explore the past. It is also crucial to understand the trading platform of interest and, importantly, how often the client (trader) wants to trade, and in which market. What works well for one client may not work so well for another.

I doubt that it is possible—using ANY system—to avoid loss. My experience has also been that though it is easy to identify optimum sell and buy points with hindsight, this ideal is rarely achieved in real time. The best that can be hoped for is to find periods of likely profit and to limit inevitable periods of loss.

When I first ventured into financial astrology, I learned quickly that clients appreciated an overview of the week ahead. This I would provide by sending out faxes (olden days technology now!) on a Sunday evening. From those missives a more generalized letter evolved (this is now my regular Full Moon letter) with a detailed and tailored report prepared for clients with specific interests.

Obviously, this highly technical work is not for general use. These reports require analysis of the client's chart, and the stocks, indices, commodities, or currencies in which they trade. No two pieces of work are the same.

In answer then to the question of "When?" do people turn to astrology, there is no simple answer. First contact might come at a time of stress. Once a relationship and rapport are established, contact is frequent. There are several clients with whom I speak every week.

How?

The last and key question, though, is "How?" The remainder of this book is aimed at showing how patterns in the solar system are linked to events in the marketplace.

In the following chapters, starting with a few basic building blocks, I aim to give an elementary overview of "How" an understanding of planetary cycles can enrich traders and investors alike. In the process, I hope that readers will share with me the wonders of our universe.

Chapter 2

ASTRO-BUILDING BLOCKS

THERE ARE A FEW KEY BUILDING BLOCKS of which I wish had been aware when I made my first foray into financial astrology two decades ago. They are as follows:

1. Solar Activity

Whatever the frequency of their trading, traders need to gauge potential volatility. In this respect, the first place to look should be to the expected solar activity of any given period.

The Sun's output is variable. It is perhaps unsurprising that bursts of energy in the Sun's surface are often reflected in bursts of activity in the marketplace. Most people are familiar with the sunspots that appear on the Sun's surface and the 11.2 year recognized rhythm associated with these.[1] Those with keen interest in space weather also pay attention to extra-ordinary bursts of energy known as Coronal Mass Ejections (CMEs).[2] These phenomena have the potential to put satellites, terrestrial electric grids, and information systems out of action. As a direct result, CMEs can bring chaos to the markets and, potentially devastating financial loss to some individuals. Unlike the cycles of the orbiting planets, these CMEs can only be forecast a few

---

1 With a periodicity of approximately 11.2 years, there are changes in the appearance of activity on the Sun. Sunspots appear and disappear with regularity. For the last two centuries these averaged 11.2 year cycles have been numbered. We are now in the concluding phase of Cycle 24. Each cycle differs from the last both in terms of length and number of sunspots.

2 A Coronal Mass Ejection (CME) is a sudden burst of energy from the Sun appearing as a long tail of fire reaching out into space.

days in advance. Even then, vulnerable areas on Earth cannot be forecast with real accuracy.

Yet there is also very useful information for tactical planning to be gathered from observations made by solar scientists. The term "radio flux" is used to describe a solar rhythm that can be forecast as much as 27 days in advance. When the solar radio flux index rises above 50, there is increased market activity. This is valuable advance information for the frequent or daily trader.

Such information can be found at www.spaceweather.com. It is straightforward to use: when solar flux is high, there is increased likelihood of market volatility. Some traders might prefer not to trade on these dates, whereas others may alter their trading strategies to take account of the possibility of unusual conditions.

2. The Solar Apex

Our entire solar system is on the move. In the time it takes to read this paragraph, the Sun, Earth, planets, moons, asteroids, and other accumulated debris of the solar system will have travelled 3600 km (2200 miles). In directional terms, it seems the Sun is headed toward the Solar Apex: a position slightly southwest of the star Vega.

It is fascinating to consider that astronomers have worked out a way of mapping the celestial skies and the changing positions of the dancers in this celestial ballet. Just as geographers use latitude and longitude to map a place on Earth, so astronomers use devices to map the heavens. The key measurements are Right Ascension and Declination (the latter will be discussed later in this chapter).

Let us start with Right Ascension. Whereas the familiar longitudes and latitudes we use to determine where we are on

Earth are determined from Earth's Equator and the 0 meridian at Greenwich, Right Ascension "begins" at the crossing point of the Sun's path (the ecliptic) with the celestial equator—a point otherwise known as the Vernal Equinox. This point in the Sun's apparent journey around the Earth is measured as having zero degrees of Right Ascension.

Beginning at this point, the 360 degrees of the Sun's path are measured and described in terms of hours and minutes. The Solar Apex holds a position at approximately 18 hours of Right Ascension. It is therefore in the first degree of Capricorn.

The entire solar system is headed toward the Solar Apex. We can think of it as an enormous magnet or compelling force.

The passage or transit of a slower moving planet (Saturn, Uranus, Neptune, Pluto, and newly-discovered Eris) across this important point affects markets over a period of months. While this information might initially seem of marginal value, it is important background information. During those periods, a Full Moon or other alignment can trigger a major reaction. Both Saturn and Neptune crossed this point in 1987 and 1988. Uranus did so in 1989 and Pluto in 2008—coinciding with the global financial crash. Readers might appreciate being reminded of the volatility of the late 80s as shown in the following graph (Fig. 1) of the Dow Jones Index for those years.

Saturn only crosses this degree (18 hours of Right Ascension in 1° Capricorn) every three decades; Uranus once every eight decades; Neptune every 164 years; and Pluto each quarter of a millennium. This information may, therefore, not sound like exciting news to the general trader. However, the fact that there was demonstrable and dramatic activity coincident with these transits suggests that the degree of the Solar Apex and alignments with it should be given careful consideration.

Faster-moving planets like Mercury, Venus, Mars and Jupiter

Dow Jones Industrial Average

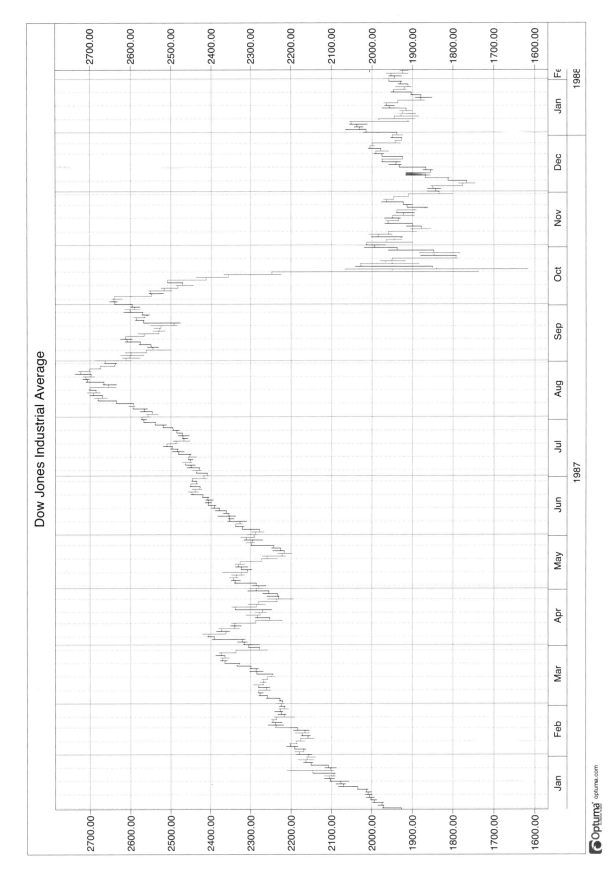

(Fig. 1) *Dow Jones Industrial Average — DJI (WI) — 1 Day Bar Chart — USD*

make alignment with the Solar Apex more frequently. The effects of these crossing are given in the chapters that correspond to each of these planets.

We should note here that both Saturn and Neptune will be at apparent right angle to the Solar Apex in 2026. This is highly unusual. The combined effect could well coincide with a sharp decline in index values over a period of a few months.

3. The Tropical Zodiac

It is vital that the astro-trader understand the difference between the terms "constellations" and "tropical zodiac" used in this book. It is hugely irritating that the constellations of the zodiac share the same names as those of the tropical zodiac. The two are not at all related. Indeed, there are many more constellations than there are signs of the tropical zodiac.

The term "Tropical Zodiac" refers to the Sun's apparent journey around the Earth. Our Sun's apparent path around the Earth, the Ecliptic, does not follow the Celestial Equator, though it crosses this twice every year: at the Vernal or Spring Equinox in March and six months later, in September, at the Autumnal Equinox. (See Fig.2.) (The starting point, the Vernal Equinox in Aries, occurs at that moment when the Sun has 0 degree declination.) The Ecliptic measures 360 degrees and is divided into 12 equal-sized areas of 30 degrees. (The term "Celestial Equator" refers to the projection into space of the Earth's Equator).

The term "Declination" describes the angle between the Celestial Equator and the Sun, a planet, or star, etc. It can be compared with latitude on Earth. The Sun has zero declination around March 21st at the Vernal Equinox after which it appears to rise in the sky as it travels through the signs of Aries, Taurus and Gemini. It reaches its highest point of declination around

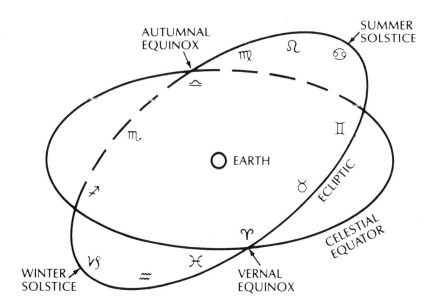

(Fig. 2) *The Ecliptic and Celestial Equator*

June 21st at 0° Cancer—otherwise known in the Northern Hemisphere as the Summer Solstice. The angle then reduces as the Sun moves through Cancer, Leo, and Virgo until it once again reaches 0 declination around September 21st at the Autumnal Equinox and 0° Libra. The Sun's declination then increases— but this time in a southerly direction—as it moves through Libra, Scorpio, and Sagittarius before arriving at the Winter Solstice, or 0° Capricorn, around December 21st, when it is once again at maximum declination. The Sun then makes its way through the last three signs of Capricorn, Aquarius and Pisces reducing in declination steadily until it arrives once more at the Vernal Equinox.[3]

The stars are grouped into constellations. The Greeks described these groupings as a circle of animals: a "zodiac." Though the

_____

3 In declination terms the Sun can reach a maximum of 23 degrees and 30 minutes. The tilt between the ecliptic and the equator gives us the seasons.

Sun appears to pass through some of these constellations in its apparent path around the Earth, it does not pass through them all. Again, these star constellations, share some of the same names as the signs of the Tropical Zodiac. It is important not to confuse them. The signs of the Tropical Zodiac are of equal size, while the size of the star constellations is variable.

4. The Cardinal Points

There are four major points in the solar cycle. These occur when the Sun moves into Aries, Cancer, Libra, or Capricorn (the Equinoxes and Solstices). These points have supreme importance for the astro-trader. The position of the planets at each of these precise crossing points is given particular attention in a trading horoscope. Horoscopes—or sky pictures—of these moments are cast for the various trading centers of the world. Though the patterns contained therein are essentially similar, the Sun might appear in one sector of the sky in New York and in an entirely different sector in Tokyo. Price levels on these key dates are carefully noted.

These charts are used by mundane (world affairs) astrologers and astro-traders alike to forecast the likely trend over the coming three months (until the next Solstice or Equinox) and have proven to be of value.

Note: An excellent example is the market crash that took place in October 1987. Charts for this event can be found with notes in the Appendix.

5. Galactic Center

While our solar system appears to be moving toward the Solar Apex—along with the thousands of other systems in the Milky Way—our Sun, planets, and their attendant moons and asteroids all swirl around the Galactic Center. This point in space is presently found at 27 Sagittarius. It moves at a rate of about 72 minutes (or one and one-fifth degrees) every century. It is thought that a Black Hole exists at the Galactic Center which might explain the extraordinary magnetism of this degree. This particular area of the Zodiac does appear to hold compelling force. It is not at all unusual for there to be marked reaction in the financial markets as any planet crosses this point.

The Sun, Mercury, and Venus will cross this point each year. In the case of the latter two, it's possible for several crossings to be made (in years when either planet retrogrades over the late degrees of Sagittarius). Similarly, Mars crosses this point every couple of years, and again, could do so more than once. Jupiter makes this transit approximately once every dozen years and Saturn every three decades—and yes, either can make this transit more than once.

Whereas the Sun moves at a rate of around one degree per day, Saturn, whose orbit exceeds 29 years, can take over two weeks to cross a degree. Saturn's transit over the Galactic Center is therefore obviously slow. A Saturn transit took place three times in the 20th century and on each occasion, market values declined (1929, 1956, and 1987). Saturn is due to make this transit several times in 2017 between February and May, but then won't make this crossing again until 2047.

Note: The Moon will transit this degree each month. The Moon is never retrograde and moves at a rate of approximately 1° every couple of hours. These hours, of course, need not occur during the trading day. It is certainly not the case that there is particular volatility every time that the Moon goes past this point—yet, should it be that there is a Full Moon on this degree, or an alignment with one of the slower moving planets, sharper than usual moves are likely. Again, if the crossing of this degree coincides with the Moon at maximum or minimal declination, a market reaction is more likely than not. This should be of particular interest to those who trade currencies.

6. Anniversaries, Expiration Dates, and the End of the Trading Year

Astro traders are well aware of the significance of anniversaries. Perhaps because significant events are so etched in the memories of those trading during days of momentous activity, the Sun's return to the position held that day (which more often than not coincides with the actual date itself), results in unconscious memory playing in tandem with the possibility of repetition.

Much has been written, for example, about the potential for a market crash during the month of October. Even traders who were not alive during the 1929 crash seem to be alert to the possibility of dramatic activity toward the end of that month. This has led to days of particularly volatile trading mid-October (anniversary of the 1987 crash) and end of October and early November (the 1929 crash).

Most important of all is that of close of trade on the last trading day of any year. This chart often describes exactly the market mood. At the end of December the Sun is making passage through Capricorn: often depicted as a goat standing atop a mountain. It is not at all unusual for markets to rally in the final days of the year. The strength of this—and how long it might last—is reflected in the position of the planets in that chart.

7. Stock Market Birthdays

Though rarely commented upon, every stock exchange has a start date: a "birth day." Though there are lively discussions as to the time of day that the New York Stock Exchange "opened," it is acknowledged that trading began on May 17, 1792 "under the buttonwood tree."

A curious coincidence is that the Japanese Stock Exchange came into being on May 15, 1878. It thus has a solar degree position very close to that of the NYSE. Financial and business astrologers often cast charts each year for the birthday of the selected exchange finding it useful in determining likely trends for that exchange for the year in question. A full list of stock exchange "birth data" is given in Appendix 1.

Chapter 3

Starting with the Sun

First Steps

You would no doubt agree that whatever you start to learn, there is always an "alphabet" of information that needs to be absorbed before you can even begin to speak a language.

Financial astrology requires that you learn more than one language. Obviously, this includes the language of astrology: the signs of the Zodiac, the names used for aspects (or angles) between two planets, and much, much more. There is also the language of trading: trend lines, turning points etc.

In this book, the focus is on the astrological language. The "alphabet" in this sense includes the names of the tropical signs of the Zodiac (not to be confused with the constellations bearing the same names) and their order. You will also need to understand what a horoscope is and the names of various important points marked on that chart. Then there are the aspects—divisions of the cycle between any two planets and describing the angle (or relationship) between them. Some of you may have already heard of the term "houses." This term is used to describe the divisions— usually by twelve though not necessarily in equal parts—of the horoscope. As you move through this book, the "letters" of the astrological alphabet will be explained along the way.

First though we will start with what you already know and translate that knowledge into astrological information.

In the West, the year begins on January 1st. The Jewish New Year is celebrated much later in the year at the first New Moon after the September Equinox. In Tibet, the New Year coincides with a different New Moon.

The astrological new year is marked by the March Equinox: that point where the Sun's path crosses the equator and marks the first day of Spring. This date is variable: occurring sometime between March 20th and 22nd each year. It is the first day of the sign Aries, the first sign of the zodiac.

The 365 or 366 days of the year are then divided into twelve segments. The start of each is determined by the exact date and time when the Sun has passed through another 30 degrees of longitude. Clearly, if the exact time and date of the March Equinox varies from year to year, then so too must the exact date and time for each subsequent sign. This is why the sun sign columns in many newspapers will show different dates: some using an average and others using the actual date for the present time.

It is not at all uncommon for there to be change in trading direction as the Sun moves from one sign to another. These ingresses (i.e., the movement of a planet from one sign of the zodiac to the next) do not always happen on a Monday through Friday. Where the ingress takes place on the weekend, the effect is not as noticeable in the trading cycle as it might be on the following Monday.

Study in seasonality considering the position of the Sun by tropical sign is rewarding. The accompanying graphs show solar seasonal effects from 1977 for the S&P index (Fig. 3), London's FTSE index (Fig. 4), and the All Ordinaries in Australia (Fig. 5).

In the case of the S&P index, losses are most likely to be incurred when the Sun moves through Virgo or Cancer; while gains are likely as the Sun makes passage through Sagittarius and Scorpio. The best quarter of the year for this index runs from September through December.

It is perhaps not so surprising that the Sun's transit through Virgo and Cancer brings downturns: it is said of individuals with either the Sun or clusters of planets in either sign, that they raise

S&P 500 INDEX Sun Seasonality Chart
Average Performance, seasons of Sun, 1950 - 2016

(Fig. 3) *SPX Sun Seasonality*

FTSE 100 Index Sun Seasonality Chart
Average Performance, seasons of Sun, 1987 - 2016

	101.8	101.5	101.2	100.9	100.6	100.3	100.0	99.7	99.4	99.1	98.8	98.5	98.2	97.9	97.6	97.3	97.0	96.7

Pisces
Aquarius
Capricorn
Sagittarius
Scorpio
Libra
Virgo
Leo
Cancer
Gemini
Taurus
Aries

(Fig. 4) *FTSE Sun Seasonality*

Optuma² optuma.com

worrying to an art form. In the case of an index, it would appear that extreme sensitivity results in downscaling.

The FTSE index also tends to move to the downside as the Sun passes through Virgo and Cancer. It does not do well as the Sun transits Gemini either. As may be seen, the Sun's transit of Libra brings probable gain which seems to last through to the Sun's arrival in Capricorn. The accompanying graph shows that there is also a tendency to increased price as the Sun moves through Aquarius, but little gain as the Sun moves through Pisces.

In contrast, the All Ordinaries Share index in Sydney tends to fall as the Sun transits Scorpio or Gemini and rises with the Sun in Aries, Cancer, Sagittarius and Capricorn. For this index, purchases made towards the end of November and sold around January 20 (as the Sun leaves Capricorn for Aquarius) have brought profit.

Using the above information alone, you could choose your index and determine an optimum time to buy and sell. For example, consider purchasing the FTSE index as the Sun arrives at the March Equinox (Aries) and selling before the Sun leaves Taurus (approximate dates April 20 to May 21). Perhaps this is where the adage "Sell in May and go away" comes from!

Clearly a strategy using just solar information can be determined. This would be a rough and ready system, however, with losses in some years being offset by gains in other years. Note too that this exercise covers a long period. It is entirely possible for the system (buying at the Equinox and selling in May) not to work for a few years in a row.

This exercise is just one component of a more complex picture.

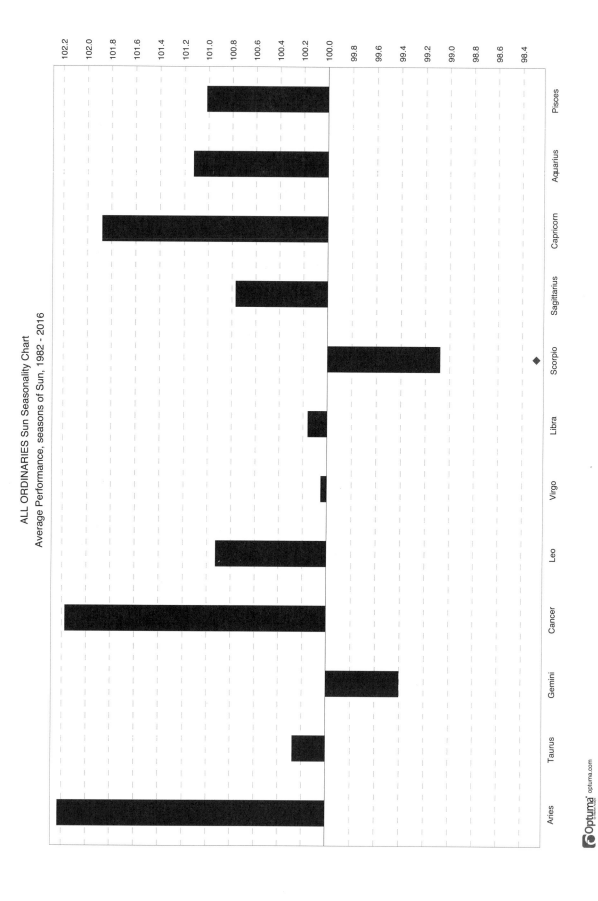

ALL ORDINARIES Sun Seasonality Chart
Average Performance, seasons of Sun, 1982 - 2016

(Fig. 5) *ALL ORDS Sun Seasonality*

Conjunctions of the Sun

We move now to considering the Sun's position with that of other planets.

During the course of the year the Sun aligns with each of the planets (though not necessarily in their order as they appear from the Sun). These alignments are known as "conjunctions." The conjunction of any two planets, or the Sun with a planet, is generally viewed as marking the beginning of a cycle. With the exception of the Moon, the Sun is the "fastest" moving object for us to consider. (The alignment of the Sun with the Moon is covered in the next chapter.)

The Sun does, of course, make angles (or aspects) other than conjunctions, and these too warrant careful study. As we learn more about the interaction of the various planetary cycles, we will discover just how important these smaller units are and the knowledge that can be gained from them. For now, though, we will focus on conjunctions.

After the New Moon (when the Sun and Moon conjoin), the next most important conjunction is between the Sun and Mercury. Mercury is the planet closest to the Sun and as viewed from Earth, makes two special kinds of alignments (conjunctions) with it. These two "types" of Sun-Mercury conjunction are termed "inferior" and "superior." *Inferior* means the conjunction that takes place when Mercury is between the Earth and the Sun, i.e., Earth-Mercury-Sun. *Superior* means that Mercury is on the other side of the Sun, so the line-up is Earth-Sun-Mercury.

Corn

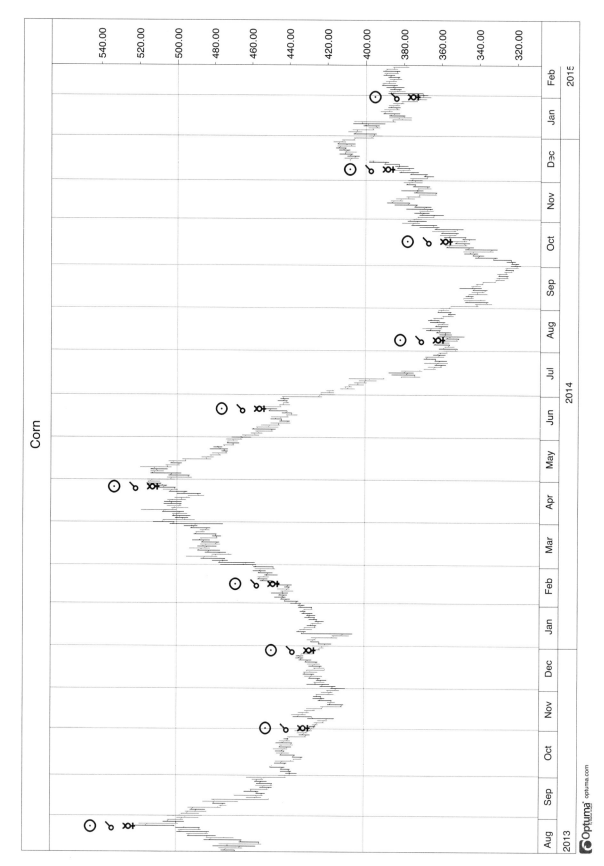

(Fig. 6) *Corn Prices with Sun Mercury Conjunctions as Viewed from Earth*

Two Examples of Solar Conjunctions and Commodities

Our next graph covers Corn trades (Fig. 6). Note that major turning points did not consistently coincide with Sun-Mercury conjunctions but that there were important correlations.

These reflect the type of subtle relationships that require time and attention to patterns to allow the intuition of the trader or astrologer to become sensitized to the influence of such aspects.

Dates when the Sun forms a conjunction with Venus are also worthy of study. In astrological terms, Venus is associated with copper. This next chart (Fig. 7) looks at the effect of Sun-Venus aspects on copper prices. It can be seen that between 2013 and August 2016, following each Sun-Venus conjunction, the price fell for some days.

Conjunctions of the Sun with Mars take place every two years and are a topic of their own. They will be covered in the Mars section.

It takes only a few minutes to mark up an annual ephemeris with those dates when the Sun forms a conjunction to Jupiter or Saturn. As we shall see in the chapters on those planets, these dates are often significant.

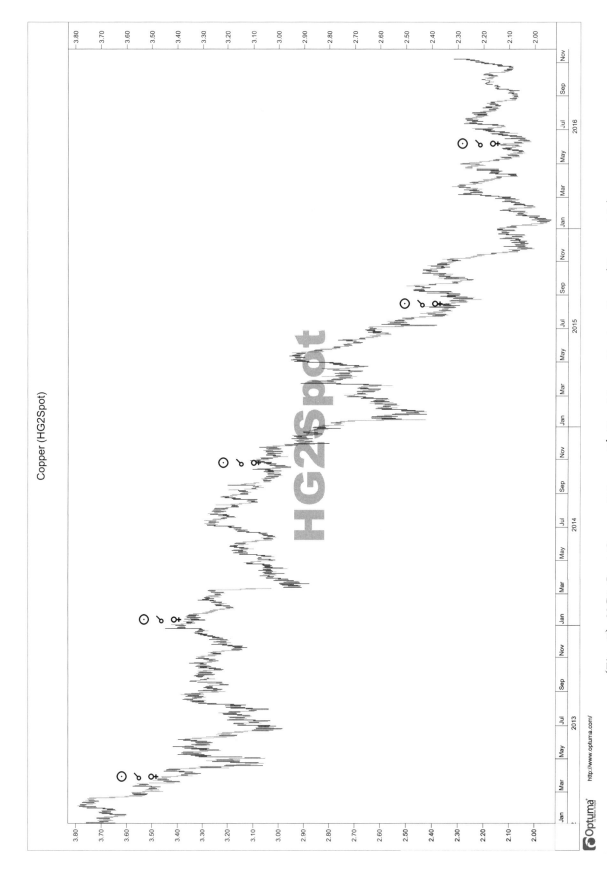

Copper (HG2Spot)

(Fig. 7) HG2 Spot Copper Prices with Sun Venus Conjunctions (Geocentric)

http://www.optuma.com/

Chapter 4

Trading with the Moon

Perhaps you have heard of lunar trading? You may even have read that the legendary Wall Street trader W. D. Gann and others (mainly commodity traders) used phases of the Moon as one of their forecasting tools. If you are already a trader, you may already have noted occasional change of trend when the Moon is New or Full. We can't know how or why lunar methods work, but understanding the basic rules of lunar trading is a most efficient tool to add to your arsenal of trading techniques.

Of course, you know the simple facts: that the Moon (Earth's satellite) is held in place by the Earth's gravitational pull, and that the Moon has significant effect on the tides and—most probably—the Earth's inner core, which we know to be fluid and in constant motion.

While the Earth turns on its axis every twenty-four hours, the Moon has a different rhythm. During the four weeks the Moon takes to orbit the Earth, the Sun illuminates a different part of the Moon in turn. The side facing Earth goes from "night" at the New Moon (the conjunction of the Sun with the Moon); to half of it illuminated at Quarter Moon ("dawn"—the First Quarter phase); to fully illuminated at the Full Moon ("day"—the opposition of Sun to Moon); and so to back to "night." There are 12–13 New and Full Moons every year.

Astrologers have long noted a correlation between emotional behavior, habit patterns, and market activity. Much has been written on the subject. A quick Google search will take you to many excellent articles. As the Moon waxes and wanes each month, there is an ebb and flow of interest in different market areas.

A report was commissioned by a major London bank that utilized lunar trading techniques with regard to the UK's FTSE index. This was an interesting report in that it considered various trading options. It compared purchase and sale at various stages of the soli-lunar cycle. The report demonstrated that had £1000[1] been invested in the FTSE in 1984, the investor who simply held position would have seen growth to £5130 over a set period of time. It compared this to the £12,116 that would have been earned had the investor bought at each New Moon and sold at the Full Moon.

If you had used this strategy in 2010, there was only one lunar cycle when the system would not have shown profit. The experienced astro-trader would probably have opted out of trading for that particular month anyway—as it coincided with other planets reaching important junctions in their orbits in the few days on either side of the Full Moon. The trader might reasonably have decided that conditions were too complex and arguably too risky for the strategy to bring success. Note that financial astrologers rarely advise or make trades using one cycle alone.

A major difficulty in working with financial astrology is that this New-Full Moon rhythm does not work for all markets. Similar results *cannot* be shown for the Dow Jones Index (DJI), or the Hang Seng, or the Johannesburg exchange. This discrepancy does not invalidate the results: rather it requires us to learn which lunar rhythms work best with which markets.

Another problem with the aforementioned study is that it

---

1   £1 = $1.22 at current exchange rate (as of November 2016)

treats all New and Full Moon as being the same. They are most decidedly not! A more in-depth study would take account of the actual signs involved and three other cycles: distance from Earth, and position by declination and latitude.

Yet this simple system of comparing price rise or fall between one phase of the Moon and another can be seductive! While this system worked well in 2010, in 2011 you would have lost a great deal of money. A review of any year as a whole—and a clear understanding of the potential influence of long-term cycles—is imperative. A simple lunar phase strategy used on its own is insufficient.

Lunar Declination

During the course of each month, the Moon moves from maximum to minimum declination and back again—a cycle that does not necessarily coincide with New and Full Moon phases.[2] Whereas the Sun only reaches a maximum of 23.5 degrees declination, the Moon, in some years, can reach beyond this to 28.5 degrees. There is a special name given to the area of declination that is beyond the Sun's reach; it is known as "out of bounds." The Moon does not achieve out of bound status every year but when it does, increased activity in the market place has been noted via increased volume of trade.

The most recent year of lunar out of bounds declination was 2006. The "wave" of declination is shown in the accompanying graph (Fig. 8) with the New, Full and Quarter Moons marked on the Dow Jones Index for that year.

There were occasions when one of the lunar phases matched

---

2 The reader will recall that the term "declination" describes the angle between the celestial equator and, in this case, the Moon. See page 21.

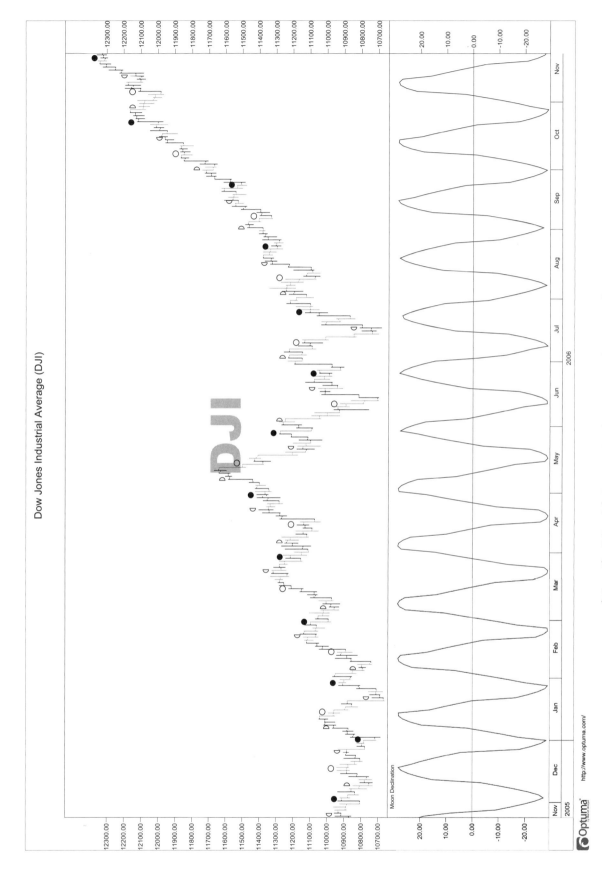

(Fig. 8) *DJI with Lunar Declination and Lunar Phases*

exactly with lunar maximum declination, or as the Moon moved from North to South crossing zero declination. (For example, look at the month of June in the chart above and you'll see that the black circle indicating the New Moon, coincides with the Moon at maximum declination.) Note the many New Moons coinciding with Maximum North or South Declination that marked a change of direction in this index. There is a natural rhythm to lunar declination. Years in which the Moon reaches out of bounds status are separated by 18-year intervals.

The out of bounds nature of the Moon in 2006 suggested that year would see dramatic activity. The next step was to identify any New or Full Moon coinciding with another important cycle. Noting that the Solar Eclipse on September 22nd was within hours of the Equinox led the financial astrologer to wonder if this date would mark a change of trend. It is interesting that from this date, the S&P rose above previous levels.

Further study suggests correlation between the lunar declination cycle and the VIX (S&P Volatility Index). The following graph (Fig, 9) shows increased volatility as the Moon reaches maximum declination or crosses 0 degrees of declination.

Such studies allow astro-traders to mark days of probable sharp movement which—when taken with technical analysis—form the basis of their trading strategy.

Lunar Distance

The Moon does not maintain a constant distance from Earth. Its closest position is described as Perigee. Roughly two weeks later the Moon will have travelled its greatest distance from Earth: Apogee. The actual perigee and apogee distances themselves vary from month to month, so that in the course of a year there will

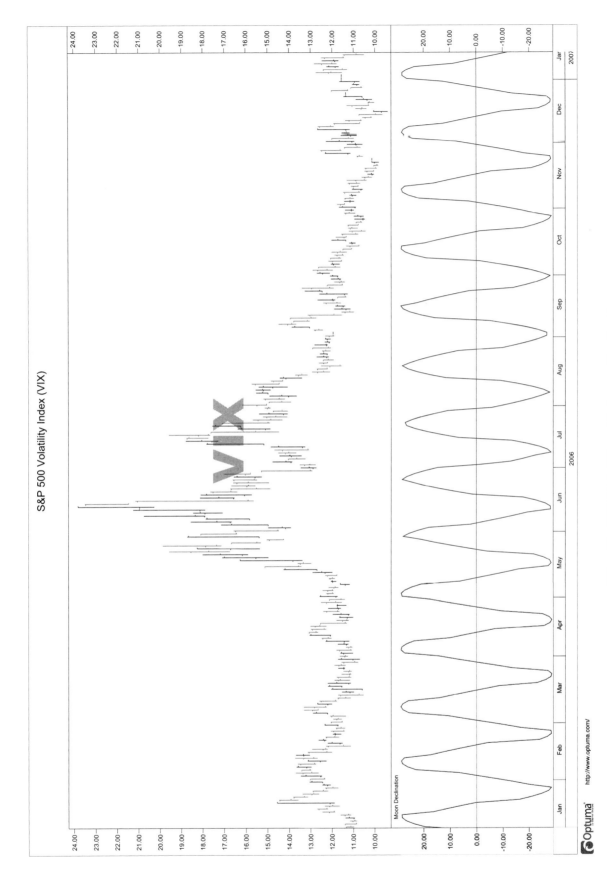

(Fig. 9) SPX Volatility with Lunar Declination

be times when perigee is markedly closer and apogee markedly further away. In broad terms, the average difference between the Moon from Earth (perigee) and furthest from Earth (apogee) is 30,000 miles while the average distance is about 238,000 miles.

The excellent astrologer Richard Nolle suggests that:

> Within the 30 hours-either way time frame, lunar perigees may signify a general excitation in living things: an upwelling of emotion, excitability, restlessness etc. Conversely, within the same time window, lunar apogee may indicate just the reverse: a sense of calm, listlessness or even malaise.[3]

This is an interesting observation implying that momentum might be lost after apogee but built into perigee. This next graph of the SPX marks only apogee positions. There was indeed a decline on 16 of the 28 apogees of this time frame. At first sight, this information would seem to not be of much value to the trader. After all, a "success" rate of just over 50% is the same as a "failure" rate of around 50%. Yet this apogee information is of use. (See Fig. 10.)

The Moon moves relatively quickly (compared to the planets). Day traders are interested in the exact TIME of apogee. Where this occurs within the trading day, markets might be expected to turn after that exact hour. Lunar apogee then is of particular interest to day traders and should not be ignored.

Moon-Jupiter conjunctions are generally seen as promising hours of abundance with markets tending to the upside. Moon-Saturn suggests a downturn. Moon-Uranus suggests volatility.

---

3 www.astropro.com

S&P 500 INDEX (SPX)

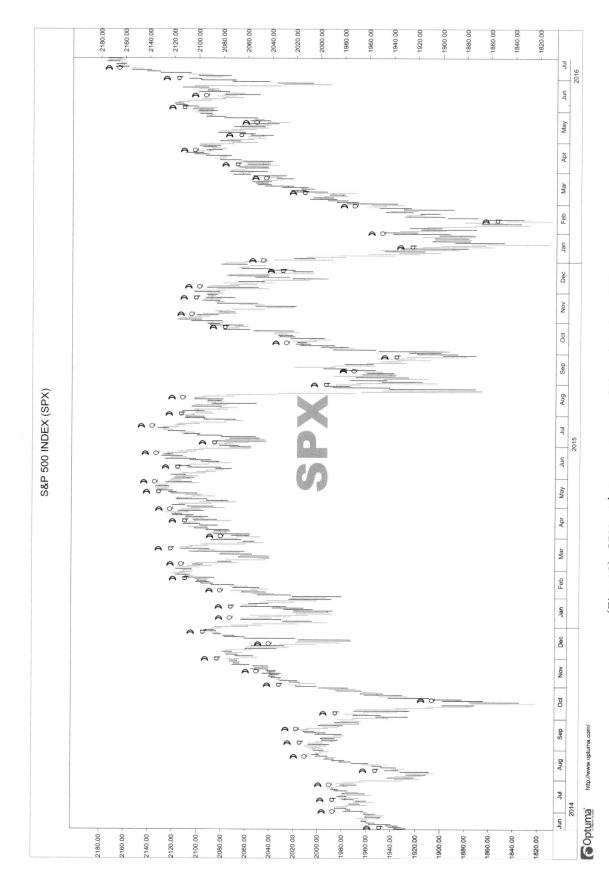

(Fig. 10) *SPX with Lunar Apogee (Q) and Perigee (Q)*

There appears to be no definitive type of movement where Moon-Neptune is concerned. And ever since Pluto made Capricorn ingress in 2008, subsequent Moon-Pluto conjunctions—when coinciding with other major aspects—have, perhaps unsurprisingly, also accompanied notable moves in bank stocks.

Where a planetary conjunction coincides with a Full Moon, there is usually very definite reaction. An excellent example is the Full Moon on September 15, 2008 which aligned EXACTLY with Uranus. Both the Moon and Uranus were then moving through Pisces. Many will recall that indices fell dramatically and that the banking system nearly collapsed.

Lunar Latitude

Another "rhythm of the Moon" is based on lunar latitude which, as with declination, moves from North to South and back again. This latitude measurement is measured from the ecliptic (declination being the measurement from the celestial equator). Again there is some resonance between maximum north or south latitude and market turning points as is shown in this next chart (Fig. 11):

We have now considered four different lunar rhythms: from New to Full Moon phase and back to New, distance from Earth, declination, and latitude. Should key phases in these cycles coincide, there is high probability of significant market reaction. Lunar planners are widely available. Here is a link I recommend you explore: www.moontracks.com.

Lunar Void of Course

The term "Void of Course" is used by astrologers to describe the situation where the Moon will not make an exact aspect with

S&P 500 INDEX (SPX)

(Fig. 11) *SPX Moon*

another planet before moving on to the next sign. This Void of Course period can last for a few minutes to, rarely, more than a day.

To be clear: during the course of a month, the Moon will conjoin and oppose every planet at some point. These cycles are important and, on occasion, have resonance with particular markets.

As the Moon moves through any single sign—a transit that will last a couple of days—it makes aspects with the Sun and planets. Unless all the planets were in that same sign, the aspects or angles involved vary widely. For example: if the Sun and planets in their different signs were spaced at an interval between 0 and 28 degrees of a sign, then the Moon would make many aspects to each of these positions. However, after the Moon arrived at 28 degrees of the sign in which it is moving, it would not make another aspect until it moved into the next sign. The Moon's lack of aspects would be described as "Void of Course." This would change as soon it reaches 0 degrees of the next sign.

Students new to this concept should note an exception to this rule: the Moon might still be in aspect when at 29 degrees of a sign provided that another planet is at 14 degrees of any sign. This would result in an angle of 15 degrees or a multiple of 15 degrees from that planet. Thus, the lunar void would not begin until that aspect was exact, possibly resulting in the Moon being void for less than an hour until it makes its next ingress. As an example, if the Moon is at 29 degrees and 30 minutes of Aries at noon and another planet is at 29 degrees and 45 minutes of Libra, then the two would make exact opposition when the Moon reached 29 degrees 45 minutes of Aries. After making this aspect, the Moon would then be Void of Course until it reached 0 degrees of Taurus. The time taken to travel from 29 degrees and

45 minutes of Aries to 0 degrees Taurus would number minutes as opposed to hours as the Moon moves relatively quickly.

Complicated as this might appear, it is not at all difficult to find tables of Void of Course Moon positions which are listed in many places on-line. (see Appendix).

It is generally agreed that "void of course" periods bring little reward. I know of at least one trader who does not trade during these periods but instead uses the time for research.

Putting It All Together

For many people, lunar trading is a good place to start. Complicated as it might appear, first list the basic facts

Determine the date and time of the New and Full Moon

Do the same for apogee and perigee for the month

And for maximum North, South and 0 declination

And for latitude

Example: July 2016

New Moon July 4th, and Full 19th

Apogee July 13th, and Perigee 1st and 27th

Maximum declination July 3rd, 18th, and 31st. Zero declination: July 10th and 24th

Maximum latitude July 2nd, 16th, and 29th. Zero latitude: July 8th and 23rd

This sequence suggests heightened activity on July 2nd /3rd and on 18th/19th (maximum declination and Full Moon). Minor effect may be seen on the other dates.

A quick check shows July 2nd/3rd to be a weekend so that any effect would not be seen until early trading on the Monday morning (July 4th). This, of course, is a major holiday in the USA, further reducing the likelihood of market reaction. In July then, the key dates would surely be Monday 18th and Tuesday 19th—as proved to be the case.

The graph on the following page (Fig. 12) is of the Dow Jones Index for July 2016. There was decided change of direction from July 20th, post maximum declination and Full Moon. This example shows clearly that gain could have been made by purchase at the previous New Moon and sale at the mid July Full Moon.

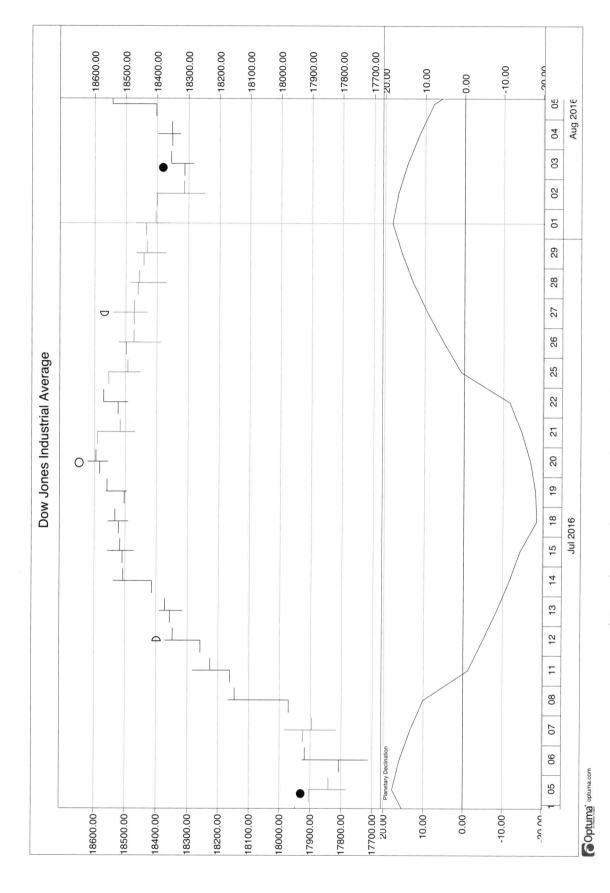

(Fig. 12) *DJI July 2016 with Moon Phases and Declination*

Chapter 5

Trading with Mercury

MERCURY IS THE PLANET CLOSEST TO THE SUN with an orbit of 88 Earth days. It has a "now you see me, now you don't" quality as it spends so much time either at the "back" of the Sun out of earthly view, or moving so closely to the Sun that its presence cannot be discerned. It is the planet associated with commerce so it should come as no surprise that its position and aspects to other planetary bodies often coincide with major financial moves.

Mercury Retrograde

As viewed from Earth, Mercury's journey around the Sun is complex. It appears to spend more time in some signs than others. These periods cover weeks when it seems retrograde (i.e., apparently moving backward when viewed from Earth). The dates on which it stations (i.e., appears to stand still, either before being retrograde, or before moving forward again) have been noted as marking definite moves in market trading.

It is absolutely NOT the case that bad business is done when Mercury is retrograde. Indeed, many successful companies were incorporated during such periods. Nor is it the case that indices necessarily decline as it retrogrades: though as you review the accompanying graph (Fig. 13), you would be forgiven for thinking so. Note that this graph covers the two-year period July 2014–2016.

In each of these instances, Mercury's retrograde station

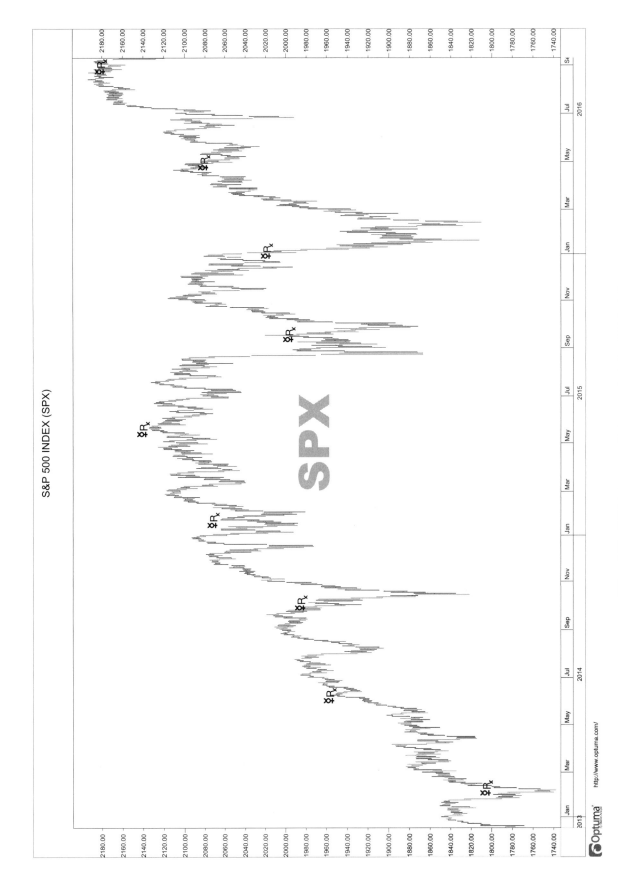

S&P 500 INDEX (SPX)

(Fig. 13) *SPX Mercury Retrograde July 2014–16*

marked the start of significant decline: which in some cases was extreme (September–October 2014 when Mercury stationed in the Fixed sign Scorpio, and January 2016 when the station was in another of the Fixed signs, Aquarius).

However, before we jump to the conclusion that the SPX index will always decline from a retrograde station, we should look at another time frame: September 2002–2004 (Fig. 14).

The results are different—with some retrograde periods marking significant rise.

Though this graph suggests that the SPX is more likely to turn to the downside at Mercury's retrograde station, it does not happen 100% of the time. It is probably impossible to be correct 100% of the time and important not to be seduced into thinking that because the SPX turns negative on many occasions that the frequency will continue. Before adopting a trading strategy focused on Mercury retrograde further study is necessary.

The following graph (Fig. 15) shows Mercury's movements through the zodiac from September 2003 to 2005.

At the left hand side we have the 360 degrees of the zodiac and the relevant months across the top: each dot marks Mercury's move to a new sign. If there were no retrogrades, Mercury's movement would be seen as a line moving from the top to the bottom of the page. When Mercury turns retrograde, there are "curves" resulting in the planet appearing to move backwards over some degrees before moving forward once more. As may be seen, there are times when Mercury crosses back into a sign it has just left before it moves forward once more.

A graph similar to this was prepared for 2016 and allowed a very successful forecast to be made (Fig. 16). Mercury was due to make its Aquarius ingress in the first few days of January and

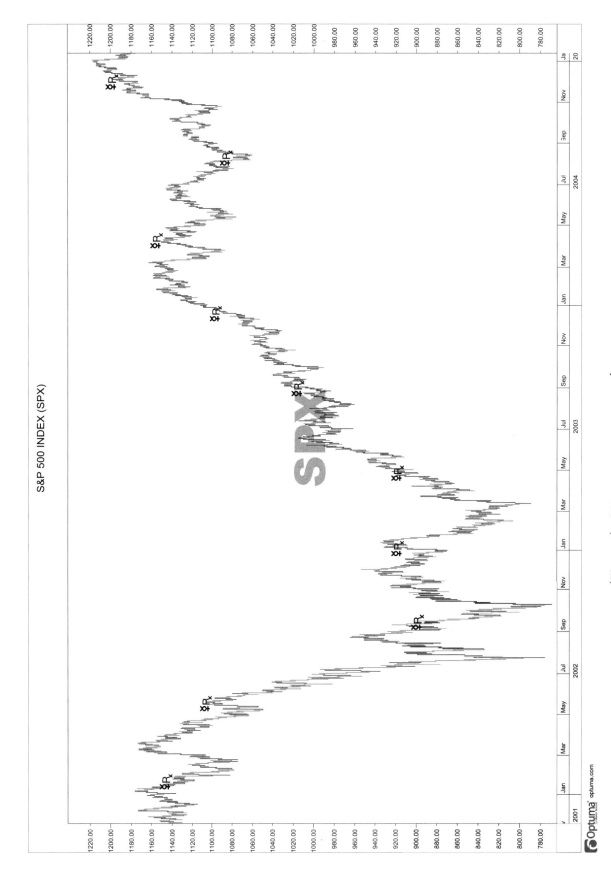

S&P 500 INDEX (SPX)

(Fig. 14) *SPX Mercury Retrograde 2002-2004*

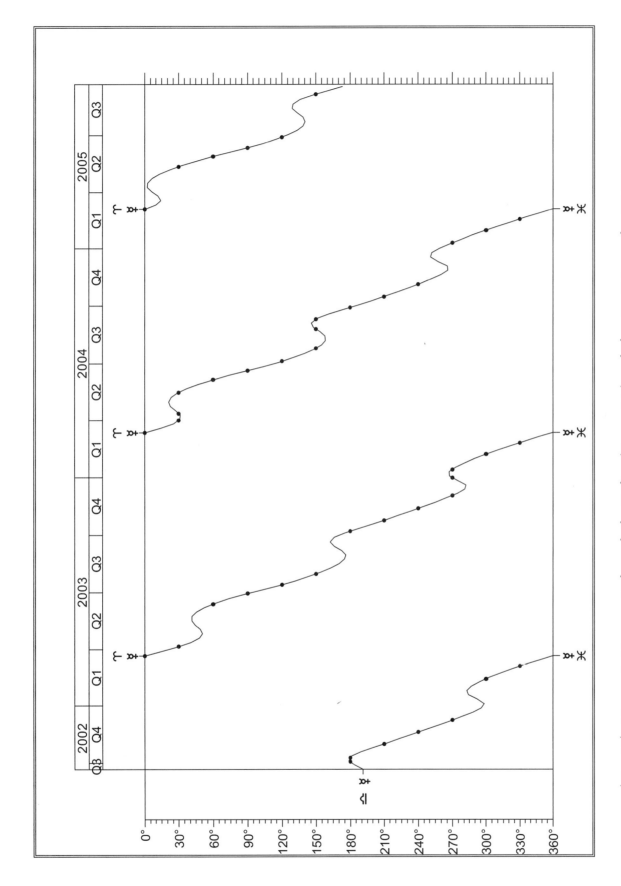

(Fig. 15) *Mercury's Movement Through the Zodiac (Geocentric) and Showing Retrogrades Q3 2002-Q3 2005*

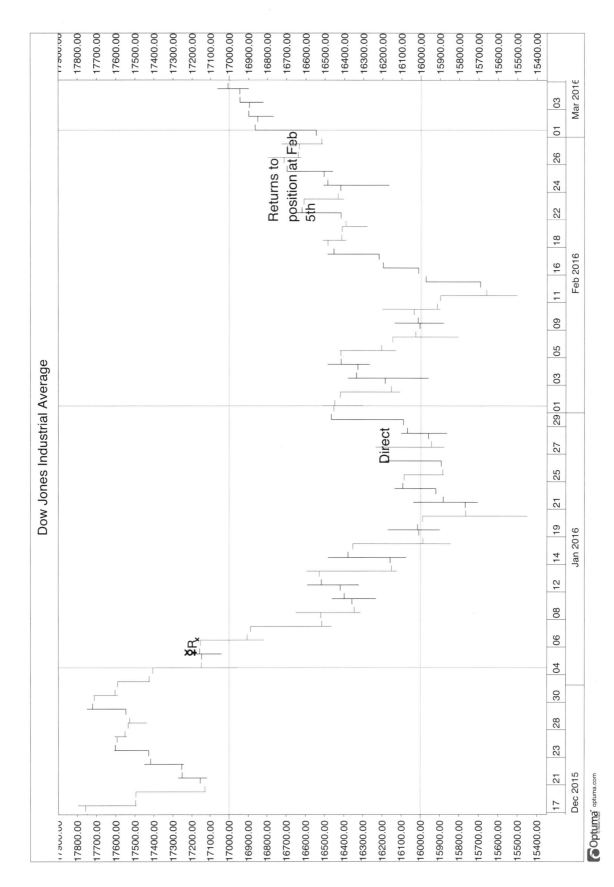

(Fig. 16) *DJI December 2015–Mar 2016 with Mercury Retrograde and Direct Positions*

to retrograde back into Capricorn in the early degrees of Aquarius on January 5th.

A Mercury station at 0 degrees Aquarius occurred in relatively recent times: 1970 when, as in 2016, it retrograded back into Capricorn. A review of that period suggested that, if history were to repeat, then there would be a downturn that would last until Mercury returned to 0 Aquarius in mid-February. As the next chart illustrates, this proved to be the case: the scale of decline being marked. Note Mercury next retrogrades from this precise degree (0 Aquarius) in 2095!

Mercury and the Galactic Center

As we saw in Chapter 1, the passage of Saturn or Uranus over the Galactic Center degree usually results in the SPX marking a top before turning negative for some days. As viewed from the Sun (i.e., heliocentrically), Mercury orbits the Sun every 88 days and so passes this degree three times every year.[1] Viewed from this perspective, Mercury moves very quickly indeed. If it is moving through 360 degrees in 88 days, it is covering roughly 4 degrees per day. This next chart (Fig. 17) shows both conjunctions and oppositions by Mercury to the Galactic center. It is noteworthy that these aspects often coincide with turning points.

(Note: In this chart, the Galactic Center is marked as a circle with a cross contained within it).

---

1 Heliocentric: Sun-centered

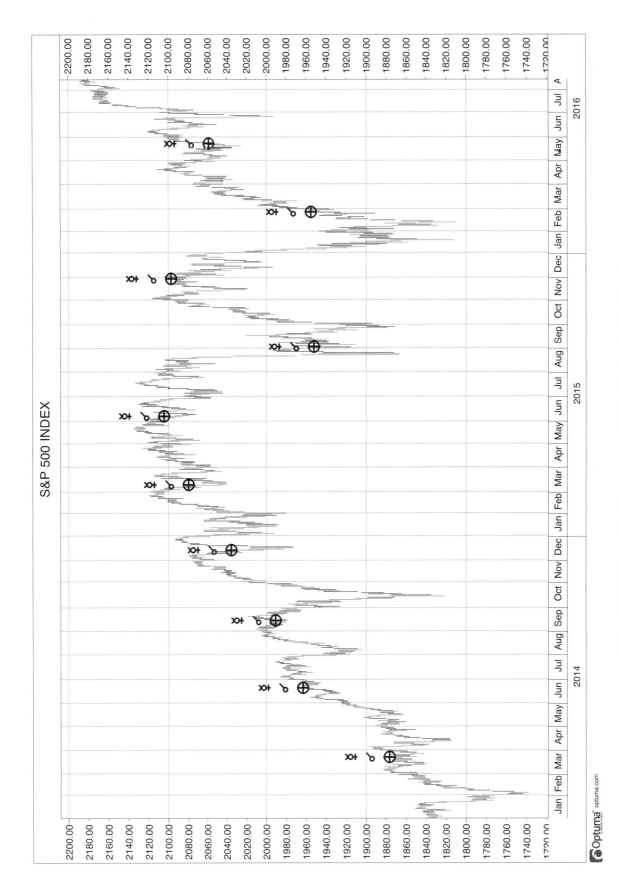

(Fig. 17) *Heliocentric Mercury and Galactic Center Conjunctions*

The Sun and Mercury

Roughly every six weeks the Sun and Mercury appear to be in a straight line when viewed from Earth. These conjunctions are of two different types: Superior when Mercury is behind the Sun and Inferior when it is between Earth and Sun. The accompanying chart (Fig. 18) shows these conjunctions against trading on the SPX over a two-year period.

As every planet draws an ellipse around the Sun, its speed varies. It should come as no surprise that when Mercury's speed is apparently "slow" or non-existent as it approaches a station, volume tends to be down, increasing as speed increases (Fig. 19).

Mercury Degree Areas

As noted in an earlier chapter, the "birth dates" of several stock exchanges share similarities. Viewed from earth (geocentric), many have the Sun or planets positioned between 24 and 26 Taurus or their opposite, 24–26 Scorpio. Mercury transits these degrees at least once each year (more if the degrees fall within a retrograde period). Volume over these dates can be seen to rise with probable volatility as a result.

Mercury and Corn

The planet Mercury is associated with the signs of both Gemini (trade and commerce) and Virgo (corn). It should perhaps come as no surprise then that there is some correlation between Mercury's position and corn prices. This is most easily observed

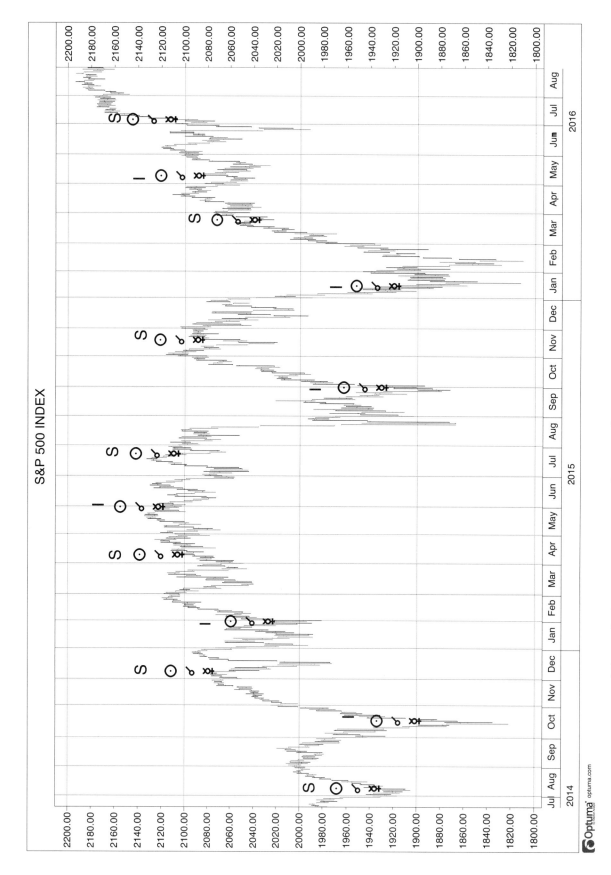

(Fig. 18) *SPX Sun–Mercury Inferior and Superior Conjunctions (Geocentric)*

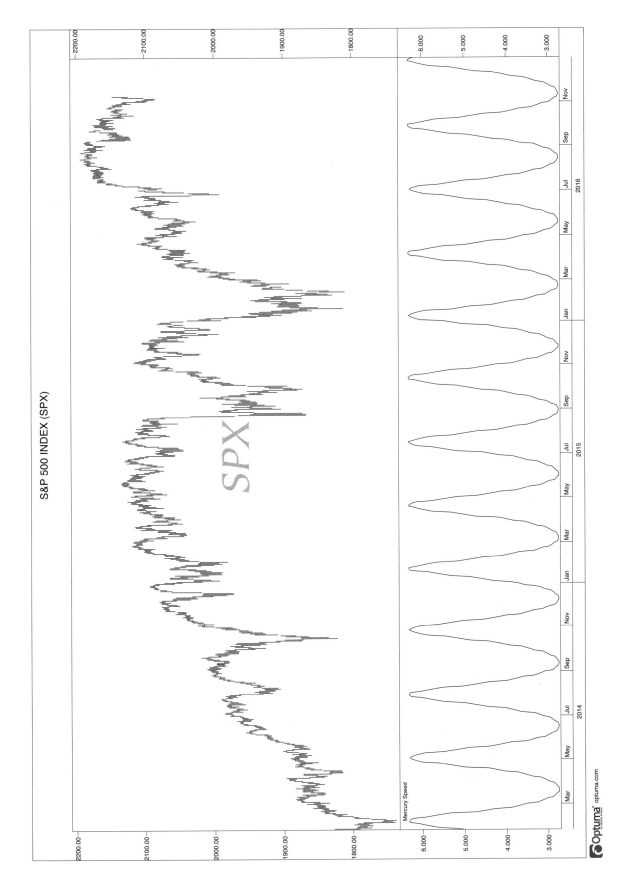

S&P 500 INDEX (SPX)

SPX

Mercury Speed

(Fig. 19) SPX 2014–2016 with Mercury Speed

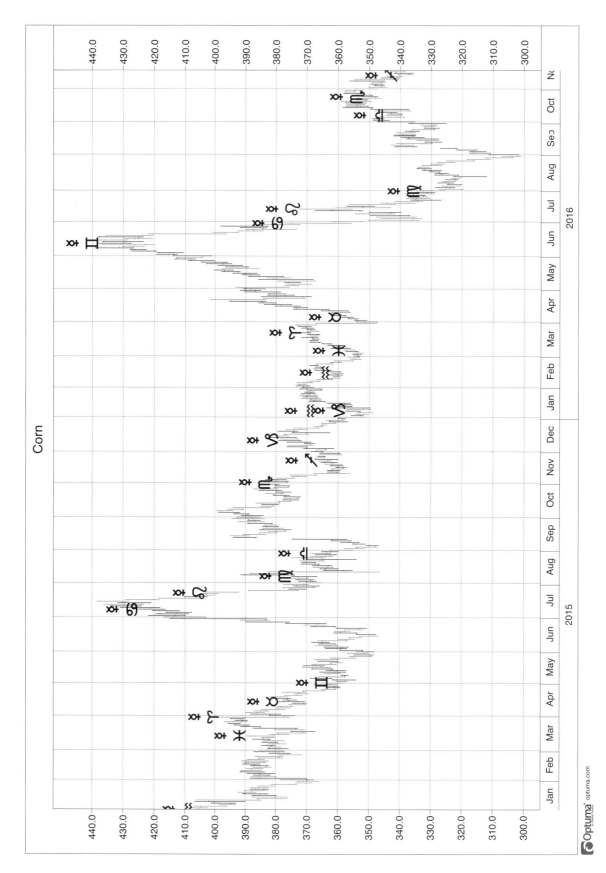

(Fig. 20) *Corn Prices 2015–2016 with Mercury by Sign (Geocentric)*

Corn

when Mercury's heliocentric position is considered. As Mercury moves from one sign to another, there is observable change in price (Fig. 20).

The picture becomes more interesting if we consider only Scorpio ingresses (Fig. 21).

In recent years, Mercury's arrival in heliocentric Scorpio has coincided with a fall in the spot price for corn.[2]

Later in this work, when discussing Saturn, we will consider the impact of the Mercury-Saturn cycle on Corn prices.

2 Most readers are familiar with their geocentric astrological chart. It measures the heavens and their actions at a particular time and location from the point of view of earth. The most popular is the natal chart, cast for the time and place of birth, but charts may be used as a snapshot of any significant event. There is another system for casting an astrological chart that is based on a heliocentric frame of reference, in other words, it is calculated as if you were standing on the Sun. Heliocentric astrology was very popular in the beginning of the 20th century and many astrologers still use it today. It is a useful tool in the alphabet of astrology and I regard it highly. It is like listening to the sound of a chord playing in the universe during an event taking place on earth.

Corn (CSpot)

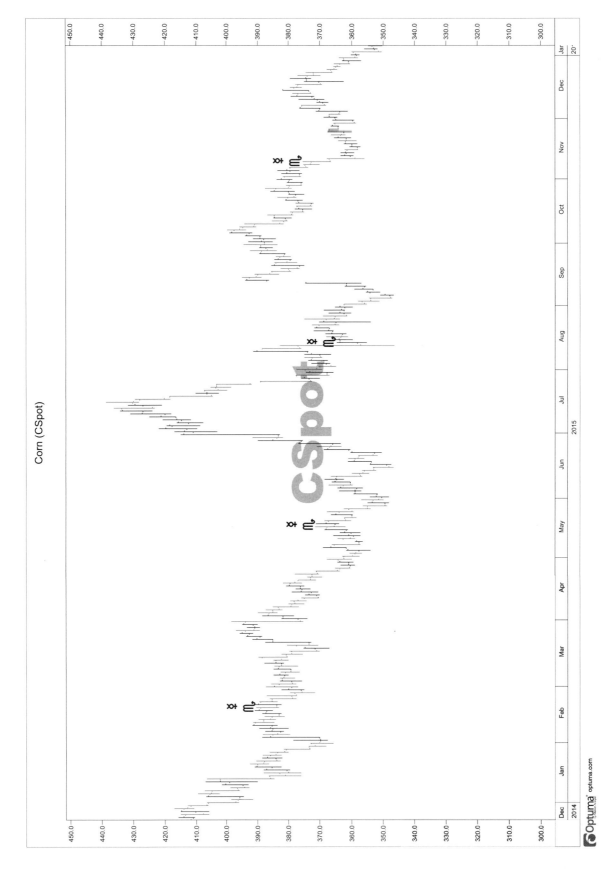

(Fig. 21) *Corn Spot Prices with Mercury Heliocentric Scorpio Ingress*

Chapter 6

Trading with Venus

VENUS IS ASSOCIATED WITH BOTH BEAUTY AND FINANCE. Venus might even be described as the planetary ruler of money. So it should come as no surprise that there is very definite correlation between the position of Venus and shifts in the market place.

Venus orbits the Sun every 225 days but, from Earth's perspective, Venus takes approximately 1.6 years to revolve around the Sun. Venus then appears to turn retrograde roughly every 19 months and is retrograde for 40 days.

You may have heard of Fibonacci numbers. If you haven't, then take the time to find out more. Few traders ignore these. Fibonacci was a mathematician of the 13th century who noted an important mathematical sequence. The first numbers of this sequence are 1, 2, 3, 5, 8, and 13—with each number being the sum of the two previous numbers. The sequence continues into infinity.

What has this to do with Venus? There is a resonance with certain features of the Venus cycle. Venus conjoins the Sun in the same zodiac sign (but not quite at the same degree) every eight years. In the space of eight years, Venus orbits the Sun 13 times and will be retrograde on five occasions: thus there is a link between the first numbers of the Fibonacci series and Venus, as viewed from Earth.

Each Venus station is approximately 72 degrees further along the zodiac from the previous one. Over an eight-year period, Venus thus marks five points which, if linked, would form a pentagram—which is thought by some to represent wealth and abundance. As we shall see, increments of 72 degrees, or half, or quarter positions (36 or 18 degrees) create a resonance—a harmonic—which can be seen to mark particular price levels.

Venus by Sign

We begin this overview of Venus and the markets with a study of the correlation between Venus' ingress dates and market activity. We need not do much research to discover something quite startling:

A review of the Dow Jones Index from 2008 to 2016 shows that IN EVERY CASE, Venus' entry into Libra (the other sign besides Taurus to which it is connected), the index has fallen (Fig. 22).

Amazing as this appears to be, and before we bet the ranch on the next Libra ingress marking the start of a decline, we must question why this was not consistently true in earlier years.

As will be stated here many times, a trading strategy cannot be based on one factor alone. The simple fact is that much changed in 2008 when Pluto entered Capricorn. If we look at any factor previous to that time, the planetary background was different.

Based on the last eight years (2008–2016) we could draw the conclusion that the index will make similar decline every year as Venus makes its ingress into Libra—at least until Pluto moves on to neighboring Aquarius in 2024.

Venus Retrograde

Approximately every 18 months, Venus appears to turn retrograde. Some years are "Venus retrograde-free." It is generally accepted that years containing Venus retrograde will contain a period of particular volatility and, most likely, decline in stock value through the Venus retrograde period.

Venus appears retrograde when Venus' speed appears altered

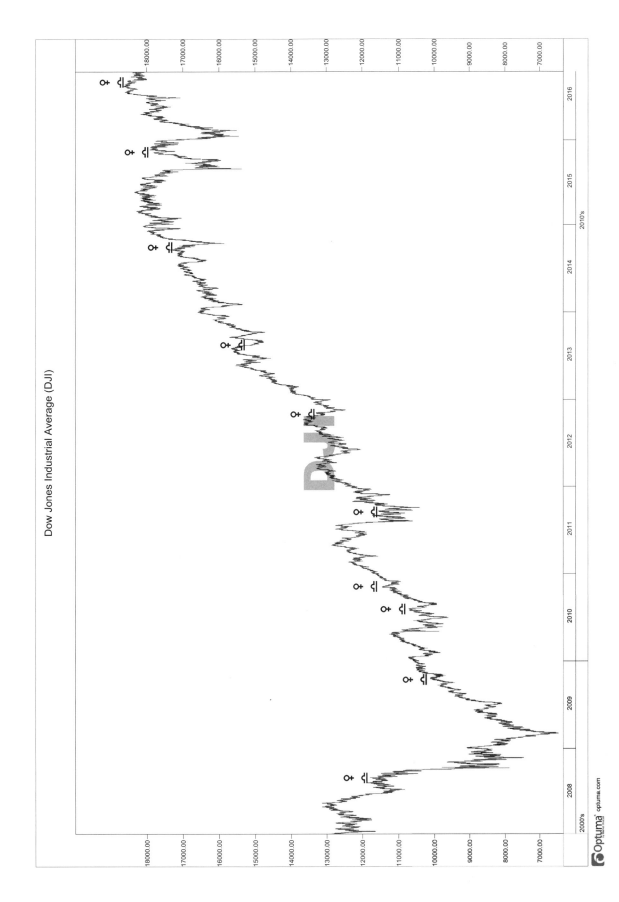

Dow Jones Industrial Average (DJI)

(Fig. 22) *DJI with Venus Libra Ingress (Geocentric) 2009–2016*

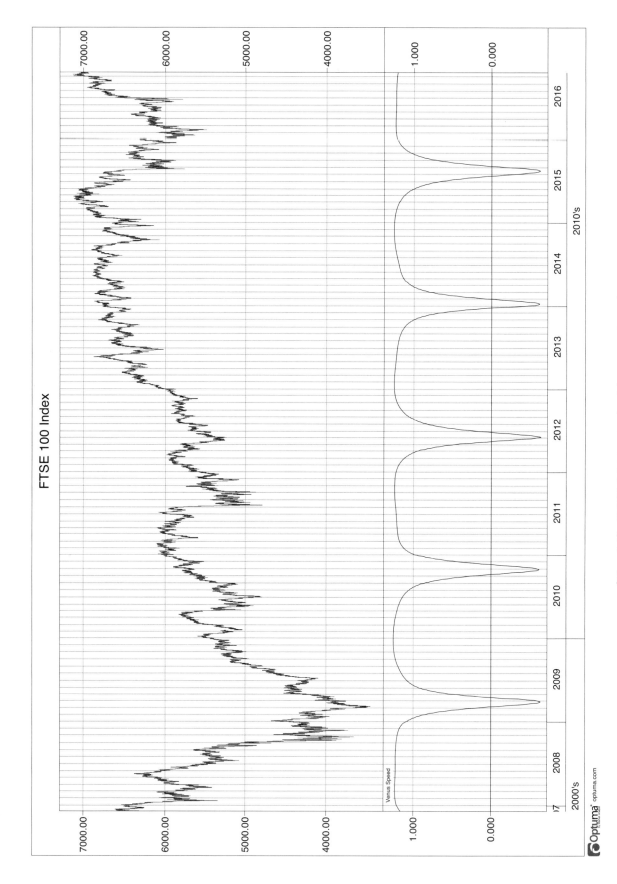

(Fig. 23) *FTSE 2008–2016 with Venus Speed*

and slowed relative to Earth. As can be seen in this graph of the FTSE over an eight-year period with Venus' speed shown below, we see that as speed declines, so to does this index (Fig. 23).

As Venus' speed appears to falter, it arrives at the retrograde stations that often mark turning points. Of the nineteen Venus retrograde periods between 1986 and 2016, on only three of these did the SPX increase in value in the weeks following the retrograde station. Sometimes the index turned negative on the exact day of the Libra ingress, occasionally within a week. Declines though have been significant: tempting the novice astro-trader to conclude that if the Venus "code" is cracked, traders could sell at one station and buy back some weeks later at profit.

As always, it is useful to look at the occasions when the forecast would have been *incorrect*. On two of the three occasions when the SPX did not decline, Venus made retrograde station in Scorpio suggesting that this particular type of Venus retrograde never obeys the rule. Before drawing that conclusion we should look back to earlier times.

We know that there is a pattern to Venus' retrogrades periods, and that every eight years Venus retrogrades in the same sign though from a different degree. A quick review of the four Venus in Scorpio retrogrades pre-1986, finds that two obeyed the rule of quick decline, while on the other two occasions the Dow Jones Index (DJI) rose. As with every apparent "rule" it seems there are exceptions!

Clearly one would be wary of making a forecast for when Venus retrograded in Scorpio. The astro-trader should double-check all forecasts using technical analysis before activating this particular strategy.

On the other occasion when the DJI rose in value in 2004, the retrograde station was in Gemini—and at a degree *exactly* opposite the Galactic Center. The experienced astro-trader might

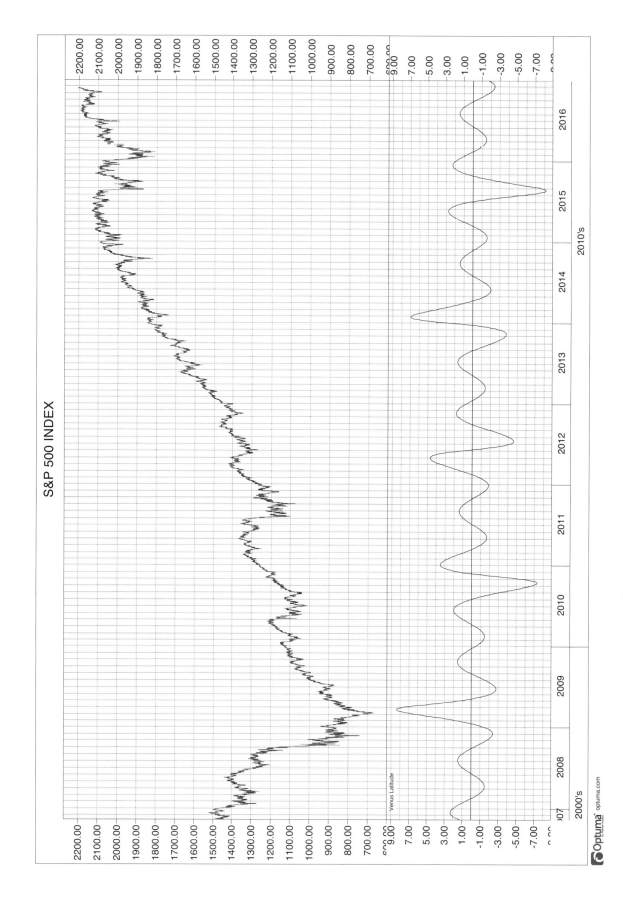

(Fig. 24) *SPX 2008-2016 with Venus Latitude*

well have decided not to use the "sell at the station" strategy: being wary of a rare alignment that might alter results.

Infuriating as it is, it is simply not possible to focus on only one factor. As was seen in the chapter on lunar trading, many positions and aspects must be taken into consideration simultaneously.

Venus by Latitude

Venus, as with all the planets, has a position by latitude—the distance from the celestial ecliptic. An irregular wave is formed as Venus moves from North to South latitude and back again. What is of interest to the astro-trader is that extremes of latitude often correlate with turning points on the SPX, as is shown in the graph below. The long period covered by this graph shows the variation in latitude values and Venus' irregularity. Note that when Venus has reached extreme latitude—either North or South— this has coincided with significant market movement to the downside (Fig. 24).

Venus and Cocoa Prices

Venus is often associated with sweet things. As can be seen in the next chart, there is some correlation between Venus ingress and turning points in these prices. This chart tracks the Cocoa Index with Venus geocentric ingresses (Fig. 25).

Heliocentric Venus ingresses have similar effect on Soybean prices. The chart here is of the Soybean volatility index (Fig. 26).

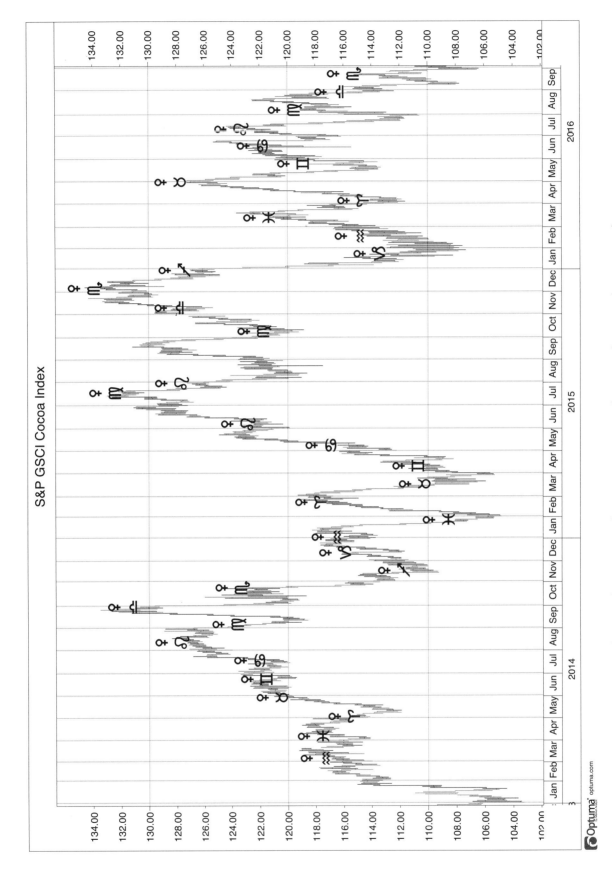

(Fig. 25) *Cocoa Index 2014–2016 with Venus by Sign (Geocentric)*

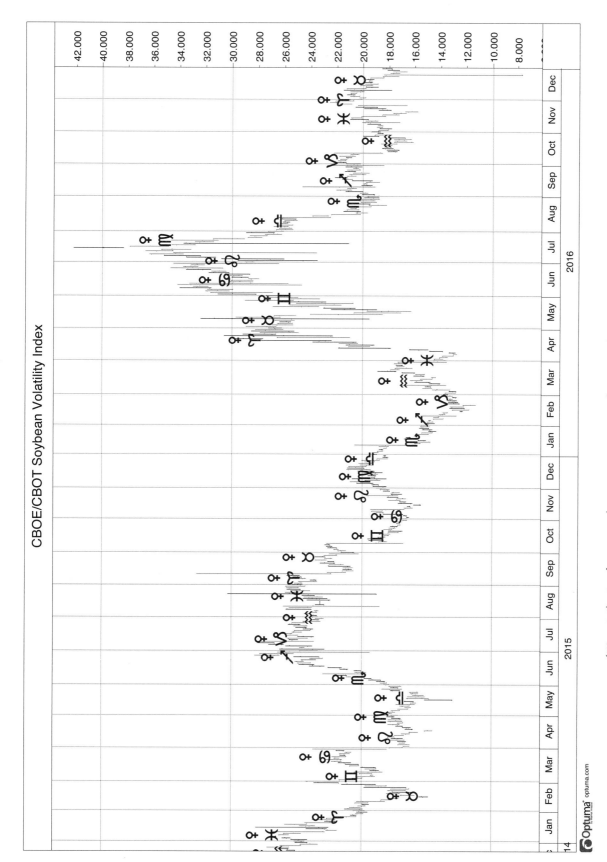

(Fig. 26) *Soybeans Index 2015–2016 with Venus by Sign (Geocentric)*

Venus, Sugar, and 36 Degrees of Sun-Venus Separation

We learned earlier that linking a sequence of five Venus stations results in the creation of a pentagram—with each point of this special "star" being 72 degrees from the next. Linking the midpoints of this five-pointed star results in the creation of a 10-sided figure with each point exactly 36 degrees from the last.

Using Venus' heliocentric position and then marking increments of 36 degrees, we find that the sugar index often turns at exactly one of these lines. This indication of possible price levels is, on its own, quite insufficient. It does however suggest correlation between Venus' position and these price levels. Taken together with other factors (both astro and technical analysis), this incremental pattern can be of considerable use to the trader Fig. 27).

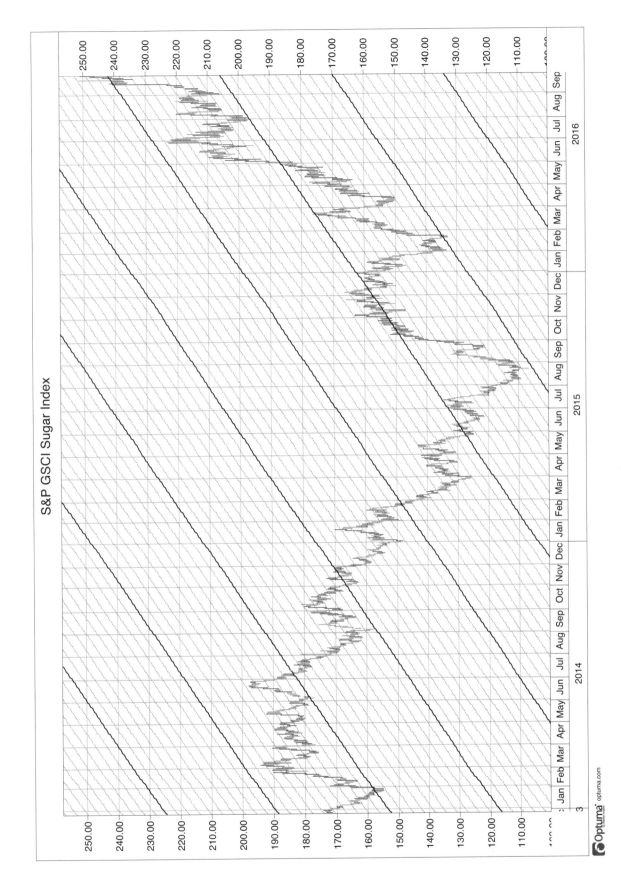

(Fig. 27) *Sugar Index with Sun-Venus 36 Degree Separation*

Chapter 7

Trading with Mars

Mars could be thought of as the "God of Activity" when it comes to financial markets. Rarely does anything "momentous" happen without Mars playing a prominent role.

It takes Mars a bit less than two complete Earth years, 687 days, to complete its orbit of the Sun—not so far off, then, from a commonly-noted 100-week or 700-day cycle used by many analysts. As with both Mercury and Venus, Mars, as viewed from Earth, experiences retrograde periods so that it appears to spend longer in some signs than in others.

If we look simply at the possible influence of Mars by sign on the SPX (ignoring the variance of days and weeks between its passage through each sign), we find that from 2000 to mid-2016, it has made nine complete orbits around the Sun.

Had you made nine purchases and sales based on Mars' position: buying whenever Mars moved into Pisces and selling as Mars reached Taurus, you would have made eight profitable trades over 16½ years.

Mars' orbit does not coincide with the Sun's passage through these signs: suggesting that the passage of Mars through Pisces and Aries, and with regard to this index, is worth noting—especially if those passages coincide with the Sun's transit through signs in which the index under scrutiny tends to rise.

Given that Mars is the planet associated with energy and movement, looking for correlation between Mars' position and the VIX (S&P volatility index) should also be a worthwhile exercise.

This proves to be the case. We find significant volatility occurring when Mars makes passage through the Mutable signs

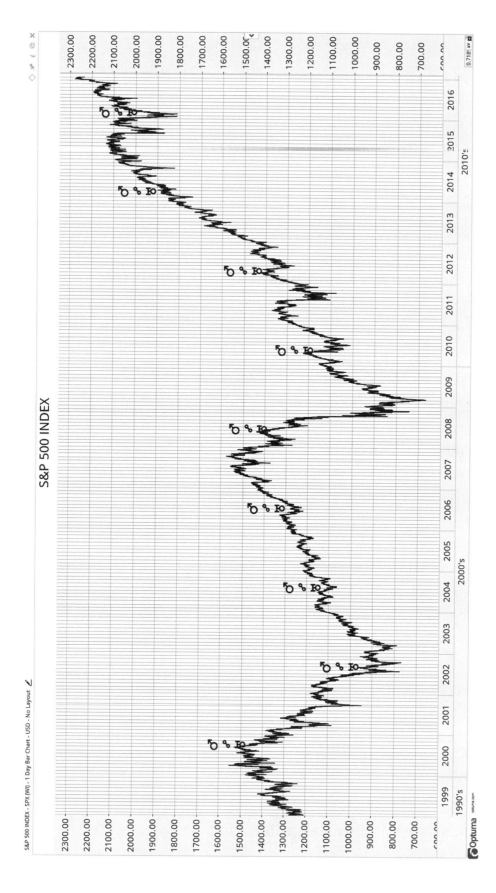

(Fig. 28) *SPX 1990–2016 Heliocentric Mars–Uranus Oppositions*

of Gemini, Virgo, Sagittarius, or Pisces. An unwary trader could be caught short during these periods when fluctuations have, in the past, been considerable.

Mars, Uranus and the Crash Cycle

You may have heard of the Mars-Uranus cycle: sometimes named the "Crash Cycle." Often when these two planets are at opposite ends of the zodiac there are surprise events that result in indices falling.

But not every time!

Again, two perspectives must be considered: heliocentric and geocentric. As will be seen, both systems have validity and both should be carefully monitored.

As Mars opposes Uranus heliocentrically just once every two years, we will begin by looking at the nine instances that have taken place since 1999. Close inspection of 2000, 2002, 2008, 2010, and 2014 is interesting as it suggests that this configuration does indeed coincide with a market top—certainly within days of the aspect if not at the aspect itself (Fig. 28).

The geocentric version is no less compelling: in eight out of eleven instances this aspect coincided with a market top. Note that Mars was retrograde in two of the three oppositions in 2014 (Fig. 29).

Mars by Declination

Next we consider Mars' position by declination. As has been seen in earlier chapters, Mars moves away from the ecliptic by several degrees in either North or South direction. At times Mars moves beyond the Sun's maximum declination and crosses into

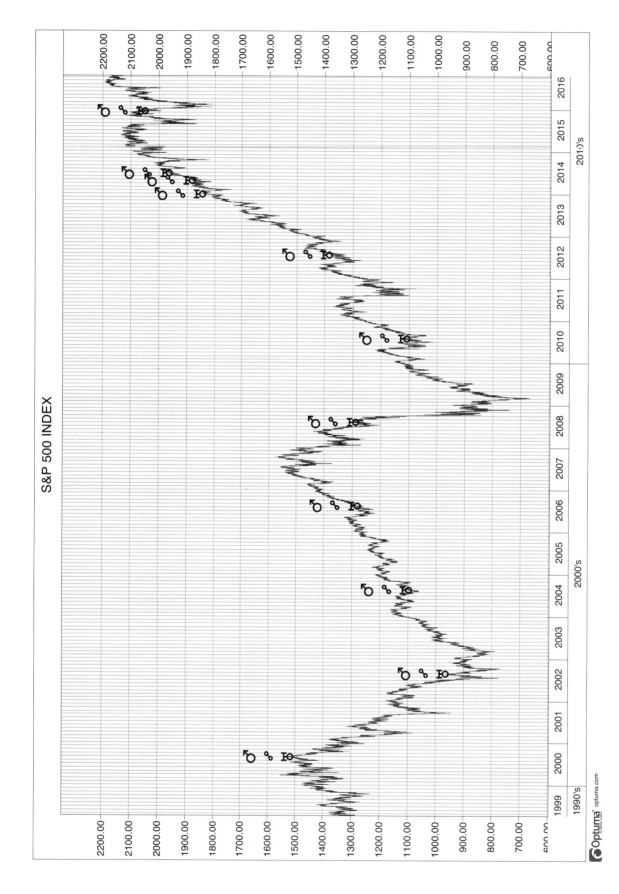

(Fig. 29) *SPX 1990–2016 Geocentric Mars–Uranus Oppositions*

a zone known as "out of bounds" (where declination is greater than solar maximum declination).

As might be expected, during these periods markets have been known to "go wild": a momentum that is lost as the angle of declination reduces and Mars comes back within bounds. Mars' maximum declination can reach 27 degrees either North or South. In 2001, Mars reached this degree in South Declination (the bottom of the curve), which coincided with dramatic market falls. It returned to this level in September 2016: once again coinciding with a low. The accompanying graph shows Mars' declination and the SPX from 1999 to mid-2016 (Fig. 30).

While it may be seen that in years when Mars reached maximum declination, the SPX did indeed see moves, comparison with the VIX (the Volatility index for the SPX) offers more insight into the correlation between Mars' position and this particular market (Fig. 31).

Note Mars' declination during the global financial crisis in 2007–8. It was out of bounds (South) in August-September 2016 and will be similarly out of bounds in 2017. Its next North out of bounds is in 2025.

Mars and Price Levels

Intriguingly, there appears to be a link between Mars' zodiacal position and index levels. Mars' position relative to 0 Aries is calculated. If the planet is at 0 Sagittarius it is eight whole signs away from 0 Aries. As we know, there are 30 degrees in each sign which means that Mars, at 0 Sagittarius, is 240 degrees from 0 Aries.

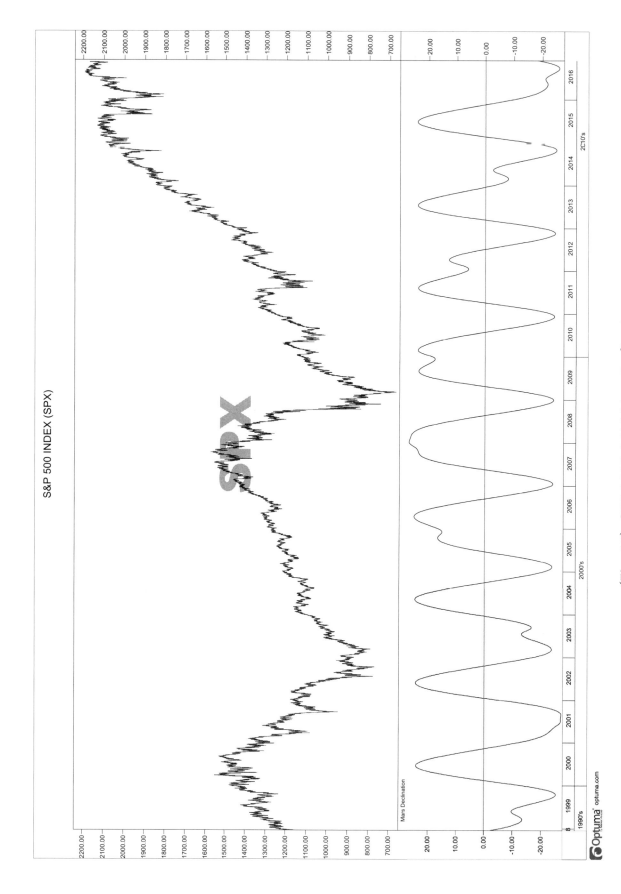

(Fig. 30) SPX 1990–2016 Mars Declination

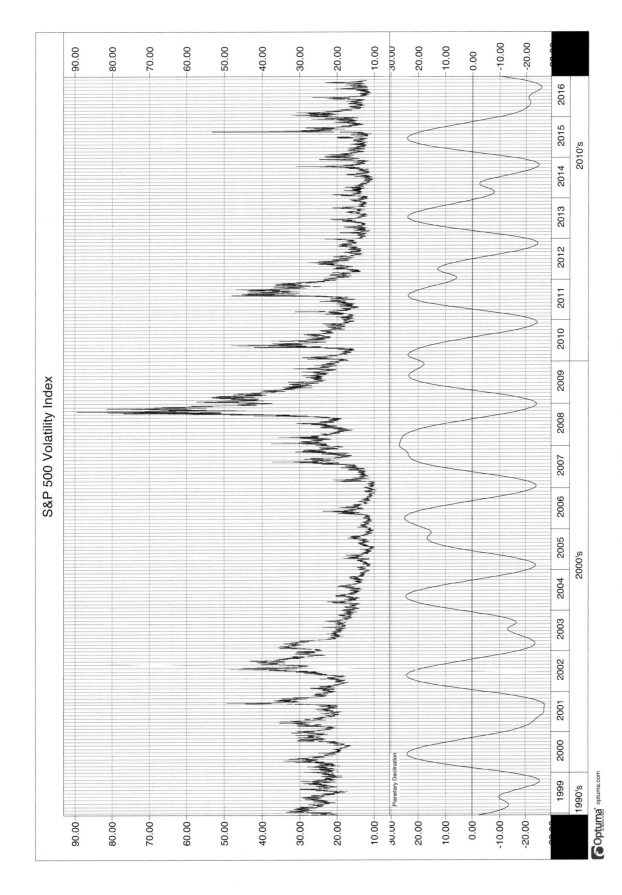

(Fig. 31) *SPX Volatility and Mars Declination*

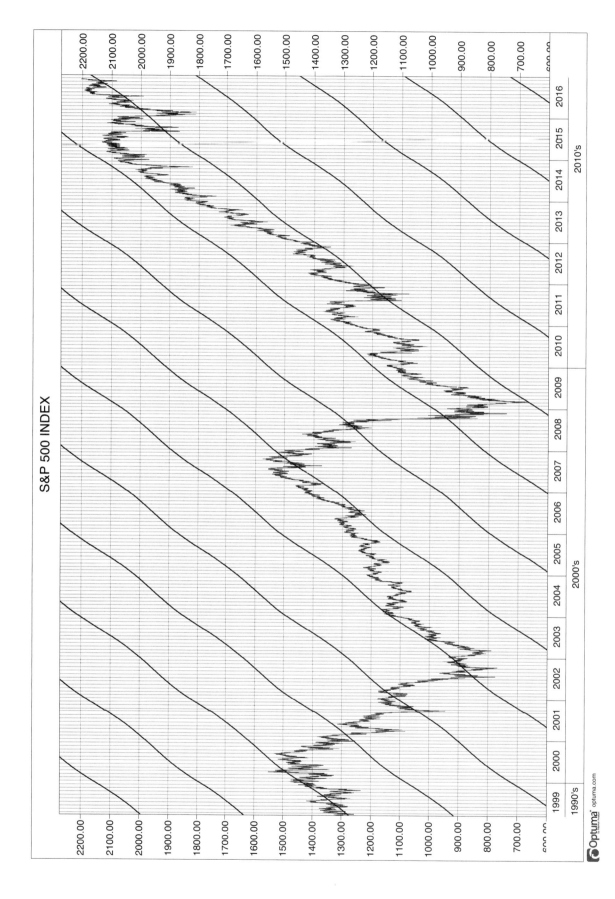

(Fig. 32) *SPX and Mars Heliocentric Cycle 1999–2016*

If the SPX index level was at 2040. This would represent 5 complete orbits or revolutions (5 x 360 = 1800) + 240. This would be our example Mars position exactly.

Another example: when the SPX is at 1892, that figure could be "translated" as 5 complete revolutions of 360 with 92 "left over."[1] Ninety-two might represent Mars positioned at 2 degrees of Cancer (which corresponds to 92 degrees from the start of the zodiac at 0 Aries).

This next chart is of the SPX since 2000. Since that year, Mars has made nine heliocentric orbits of the Sun. Each of its orbits is marked by a black line. Note how the low in 2008 coincided with the Mars line. Using these simple Mars positions is useful but, as always, only part of the story (Fig. 32):

It is usual for the experienced astro-trader to consider what might be termed "mirror" positions, i.e. working with 180, or 90, or 60 or even 15 degree increments from the actual Mars position. When this is done, the results offer compelling information.

To show just how useful this information can be, this next graph is of the SPX in 2015 with 15 degree increments marked. Though this is insufficient information on which to trade, supported by technical analysis it offers clues as to likely turning point levels (Fig. 33).

Of course, it would be quite wrong to say that the index level marked by Mars is the only factor to be considered. When the position of other planets, their relationship to one another, and the Sun-Moon cycle are factored in with this, the astro-trader is provided with very useful information indeed. We will look at the interaction of Mars with outer planet cycles later.

---

1   5 x 360 = 1800 + 92 = 1892.

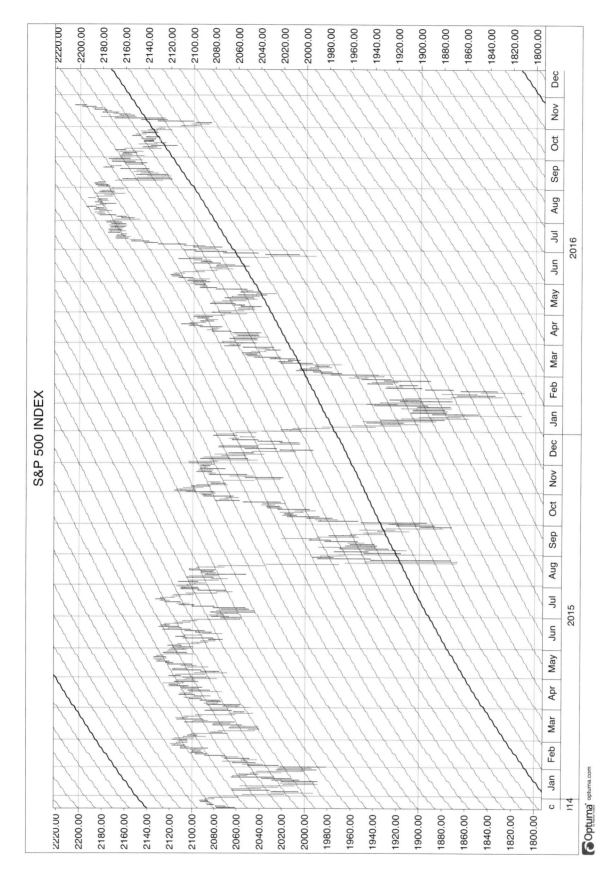

(Fig. 33) *SPX Mars Heliocentric 2015-2016 with 15 Degree Increment*

Mars and Forex

An area of particular interest to the astro-trader relates to Mars' movements with regard to Forex (foreign exchange) trading. Some very interesting research has already been carried out in this area. As always, more work needs to be done but, so far, early results show promise.

There is one well-documented period between high and low in Euro-USD trading that had the exact length of a Mars cycle. The length of Mars' orbit is 1.81 Earth years or 780 days. This is the time it takes for Mars to appear (as viewed from Earth) to oppose the Sun and then to continue its travels until it reaches its next opposition to the Sun—its synodic cycle. The Euro reached low points with the dollar on June 4, 2010 and July 24, 2012: those lows being exactly 779 days apart.

Note that this example does not "start" with Mars at 0 Aries, but later in the zodiac—in the first degree of Virgo. As we saw with the SPX example, it is not unusual for a change of trend to occur when Mars reaches a new ingress. What we might note here is that the sign involved is Virgo. Planetary activity in this area of the zodiac often sees major fluctuations in currency exchanges.

Note too that on neither June 4, 2010 nor July 24, 2012 was the Sun in exact opposition to Mars. Even so, the fact that there is direct relationship between the number of days between these two lows and the length of Mars' synodic cycle suggests a "Mars' factor" worthy of closer attention.

On the former date Mars (geocentrically) had just reached Virgo while the Sun was still moving through Gemini. There was an angular relationship of 73 degrees between the two (from the Sun at 17 Gemini to Mars at 0 Virgo geocentric positions). Seven hundred seventy-nine days later, the Sun had just entered Leo while Mars was at 11 degrees of Libra. This time, the two were approximately 72 degrees apart (again with the Sun "behind" Mars). Seventy-two degrees is exactly one fifth of a circle of 360 degrees (a quintile).

Research was then carried out to ascertain if the occasions when the Sun and Mars were at either 72, 144, 216, or 288 degrees (fifth or multiple fifths of a circle apart). While not every significant turning point was revealed for the period under review, several dates seem to suggest that there might indeed be a resonance between Sun-Mars quintile aspects and this particular currency exchange.

Chapter 8

Trading with Jupiter

IT TAKES JUPITER 11.88 EARTH YEARS TO ORBIT THE SUN: as a result
of which it spends roughly a year in each sign. However, as with
all the planets, its orbit is not a perfect circle but an ellipse. It
spends rather longer in some signs than others depending on its
distance relative to the Sun. As viewed from Earth, in every year
there will be weeks when Jupiter is in apparent retrograde motion.
The stations, i.e. those dates when it appears to be standing still
in the sky, are dates to note.

So, too, are those dates when the Sun and Jupiter appear in
alignment (conjunction) or are perhaps a third of a circle apart
(trine). In certain cultures such dates are chosen for marriage
celebrations. Gold traders have noted that the price of gold tends
to rise in the days leading into these important aspects.

Traders have been known to overreact as this planet moves
from one zodiac sign to another. Astrologers do not find this
surprising. Since this planet is the largest in the known solar
system, it is associated with exaggeration.

It would, of course, be convenient if Jupiter made each
ingress on the first day of the year. The dates of ingresses vary
enormously, making it necessary to check the ephemeris. Also,
remember that as Jupiter is retrograde for some weeks every year,
it is always possible that it will return to a sign before making a
second and last ingress. Each of these dates should be noted.

As before, we start by considering the effect of Jupiter moving
through each sign. For this example, using the SPX, and observing
one-and-a-half complete orbits of Jupiter (from Aries to the next
Aries is one complete journey through the twelve signs and on

S&P 500 INDEX (SPX)

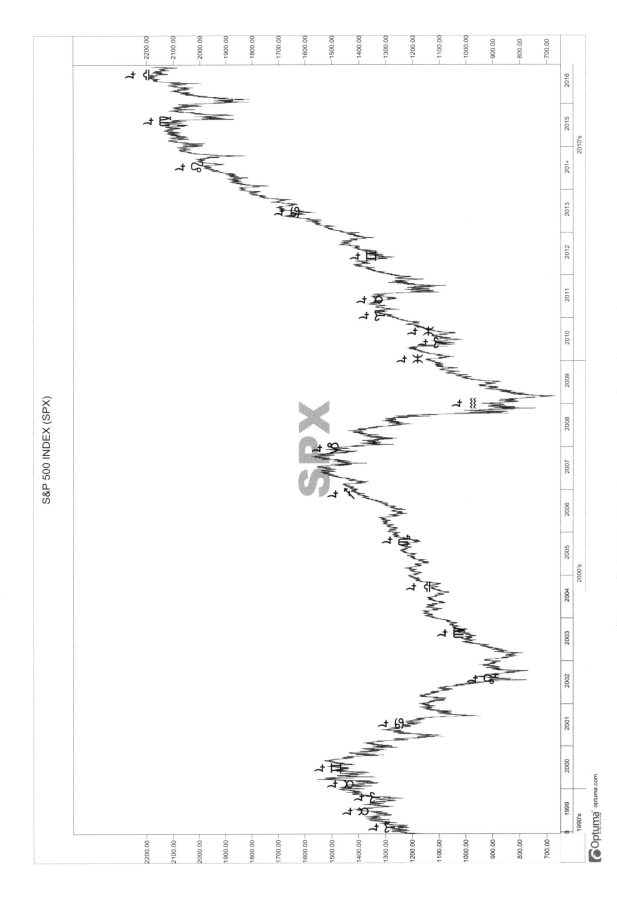

(Fig. 34) SPX Jupiter Geocentric Cycle and Sign Changes

through Virgo to Libra for a total of 18 sign changes). Note the immediate effect of the falling index as Jupiter made both Aquarius and Pisces ingress (Fig. 34).

Note that when Jupiter moved through Cancer in 2001, the index fell. Its next move through that sign in 2013 witnessed a rise. The point to make here is that a judgement or rule cannot be obtained by sign alone, but that there is clear value to the trader in being aware of these key dates. If technical indicators concur, a trading strategy for these periods can be put in place.

On Tuesday, August 11, 2015, Jupiter made geocentric Virgo ingress as the Moon reached maximum declination for the month: most likely exaggerating any effect. Over the course of the weekend prior to this ingress, both Mercury and Mars changed sign. It was expected, then, with three planets in new signs and a high of lunar declination, a change of mood would operate in the markets, and that this shift would be reflected in sharp moves (Fig. 35).

Jupiter Retrograde

Jupiter has a retrograde period each year. Stocks which lose value sharply at the retrograde station often recover as quickly when Jupiter turns direct. Indeed, the watchful trader can build profit by purchasing at a low (perhaps derived through technical analysis) during Jupiter's retrograde period.

The example given here is of Alphabet (formerly Google) trading in 2015 (Fig. 36).

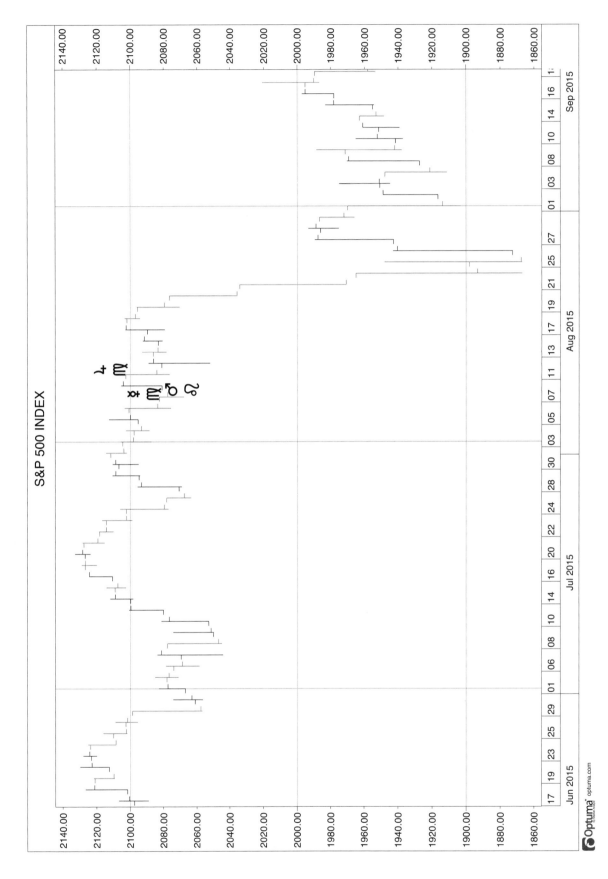

S&P 500 INDEX

(Fig. 35) *SPX August 2015 with Mercury, Mars and Jupiter Sign Change*

Alphabet Inc

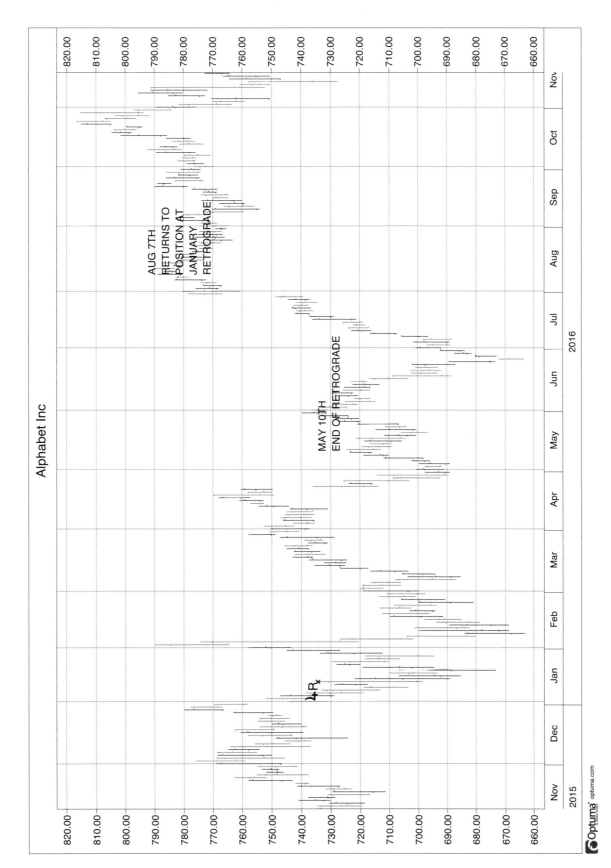

AUG 7TH
RETURNS TO
POSITION AT
JANUARY
RETROGRADE

MAY 10TH
END OF RETROGRADE

♃ Rx

(Fig. 36) *Alphabet (Google) Jupiter Retrograde 2016*

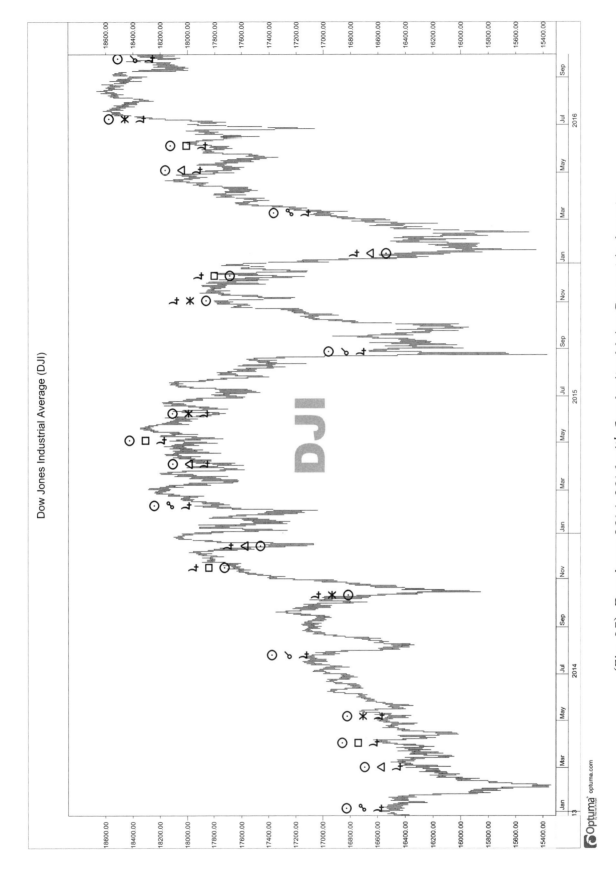

Dow Jones Industrial Average (DJI)

(Fig. 37) *Dow Jones 2014–2016 with Sun Jupiter Major Geocentric Aspects*

Jupiter and the Sun

Aspects between the Sun and Jupiter are traditionally deemed "good" and it is typical for such dates to be chosen for weddings or feast days. These dates will vary from year to year. Generally, days when the Sun is either conjunct Jupiter or at a multiple of 60 degrees (sextile) from it, are thought to be "blessed." Note that this list includes the 180 degree opposition aspect, which some see as being "negative" but which often coincides with a market top. This next chart covers two years of the DJI with the main Sun-Jupiter (geocentric) aspects marked. The results are indeed interesting. Note how this index rose on the day of the Sun-Jupiter conjunction in August 2015. This aspect came a few days after the decline that coincided with Jupiter's Virgo ingress (Fig. 37).

Some research has been done on the link between Sun-Jupiter aspects and the price of gold. David Cochrane and his team found a compelling link between a rise in the gold price when the Sun and Jupiter were multiples of 51 degrees and 20 minutes apart (seventh of a circle).

This next chart (Fig. 38) marks these and other Sun Jupiter aspects on the XAUUSD (Gold-US dollar index).

There is tempting correlation between highs in this index and Sun-Jupiter aspects. Particularly noteworthy are the highs (sometimes major) when the Sun and Jupiter are either at 51, 60, or 150 degrees of separation.

Could these turning points have been forecast?

Even with early/beginner knowledge, the answer must surely be "yes."

The combination of Sun-Jupiter opposition just ahead of the New Moon—and falling between Mars' Sagittarius ingress and Venus' move into Pisces—suggested a turning point, as proved to

Gold / US Dollar (XAUUSD)

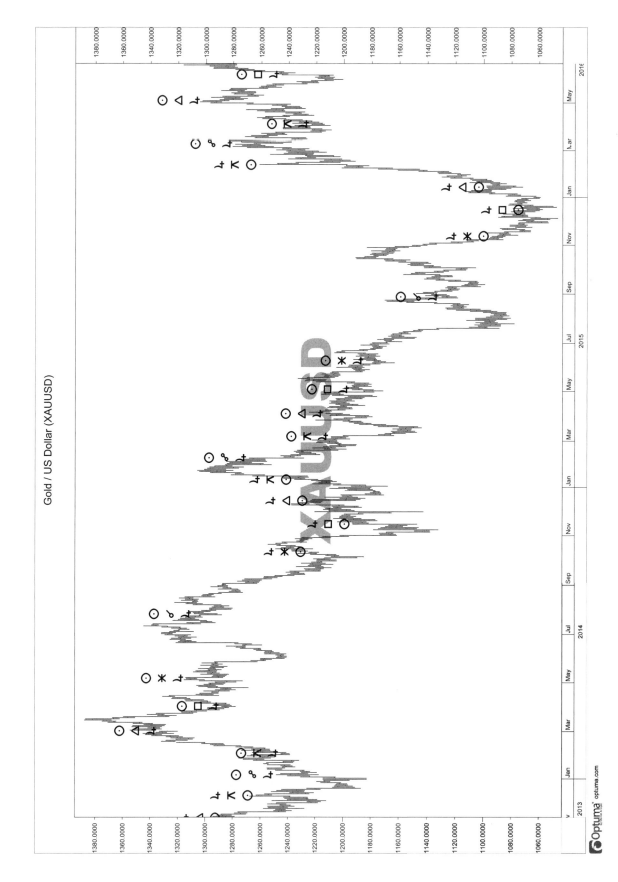

(Fig. 38) *Gold/USD Dollar 2014–2016 with Major Sun–Jupiter Geocentric Aspects*

be the case. The experienced astro-trader might well have decided to sell after Mars' made that Sagittarius ingress and before the opposition.

Equally it might have been anticipated that the 150 degree aspect (quincunx) between the Sun and Jupiter just ahead of Venus' move into Aries, would likely form another turning point (Fig. 39).

Assuming that purchase was made in early April, when then best to sell?

The combination of Venus' next ingress (Taurus) again—just ahead of the Sun's 120 degree (trine) to Jupiter itself ahead of the New Moon—would suggest sale between the ingress and the Sun-Jupiter trine.

Given the high probability that the Sun-Jupiter sextile in July, two days ahead of Venus' Leo ingress (and another change of mood), the astro-trader would then look for a buy signal ahead of this aspect. The answer to this requires understanding of another major cycle—Jupiter and Saturn had reached their quarter phase when the two planets are a quarter of a cycle apart (90 degrees).

The sharp move between this aspect and the 90 degree (square) angle between the Sun and Jupiter brought gain for those poised to seize this opportunity.

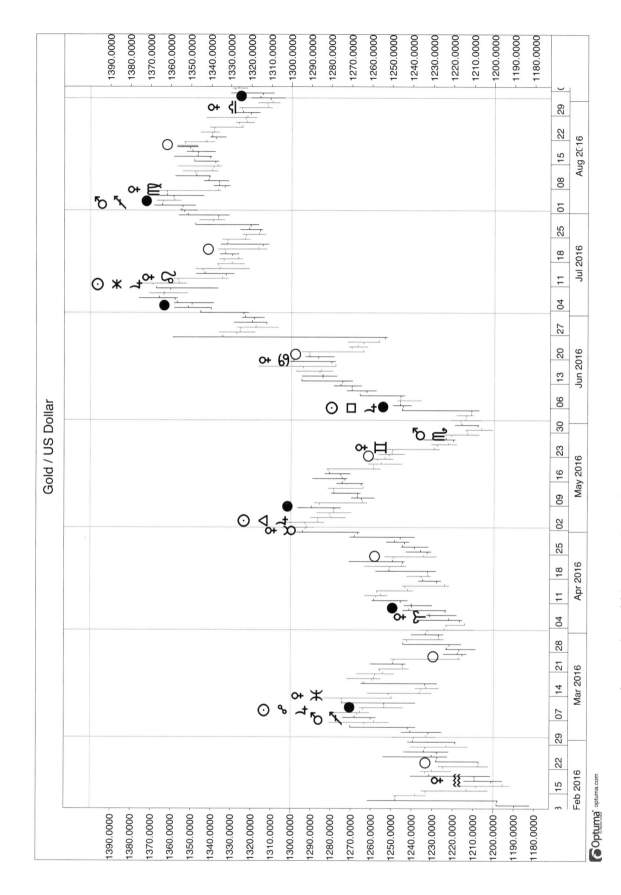

Gold / US Dollar

(Fig. 39) *Gold/USD Dollar Feb 2016–August 2016 Major Geocentric Factors*

Chapter 9

Trading with Saturn

Saturn takes over 29 years to orbit the Sun and spends around two-and-a-half years in each sign. The traditional astrological perspective is that Saturn presents a boundary: a line which should not be crossed. It is also associated with the sign of Capricorn which is often depicted as a goat at the top of a mountain. Saturn can indeed mark a "highest point." There are many examples—across many markets—when Saturn's change of sign marks a market top.

Yet Saturn is also associated with the "bottom line": a low point. Whether marking a top or a bottom, a strong Saturn position marks a boundary. That "strong" position can be defined by a Saturn ingress, a New or Full Moon aligning with Saturn, or a conjunction of Saturn with the Sun or another planet.

In the following graph (Fig. 40), it can be seen clearly that from Saturn's Scorpio ingress, the price of gold against the US dollar coincided with a peak from which the price declined. This is, perhaps, unsurprising as Saturn can act as a depressant. Scorpio is the sign most associated with mining. It is interesting to note that there was some immediate recovery as Saturn moved into Sagittarius—though that was not sustained.

Saturn ingresses compared with other markets should also be considered.

This next chart (Fig. 41) offers an entire Saturn cycle, showing clearly that the passage through both Gemini and Virgo (the two signs ruled by Mercury), saw significant decline.

The effect of Saturn's transits on the Hang Seng index is a little different: as can be seen below (Fig. 42). Saturn's transits

Gold / US Dollar (XAUUSD)

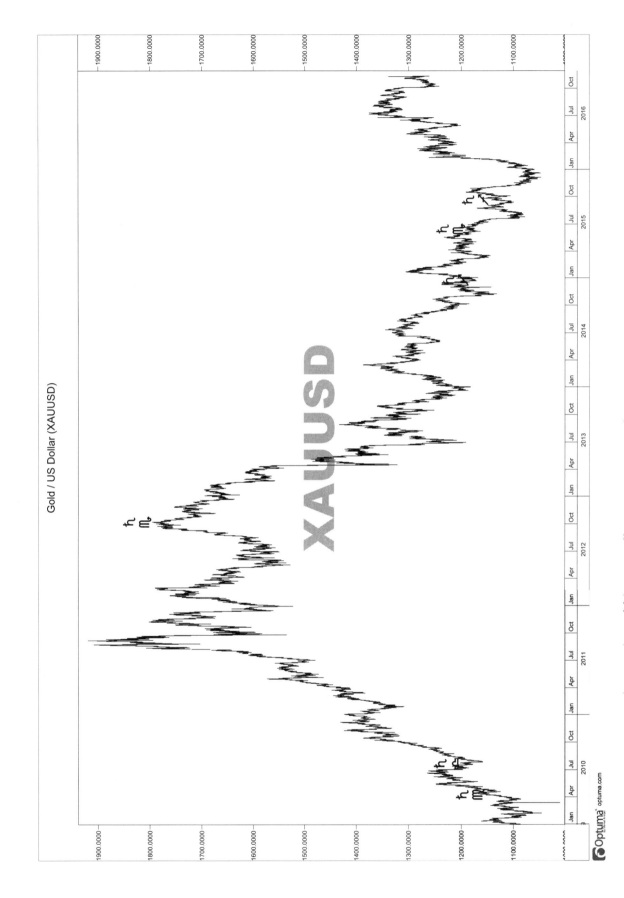

(Fig. 40) *Gold/USD Dollar 2011-2016 with Saturn Scorpio Geocentric Ingress*

S&P 500 INDEX (SPX)

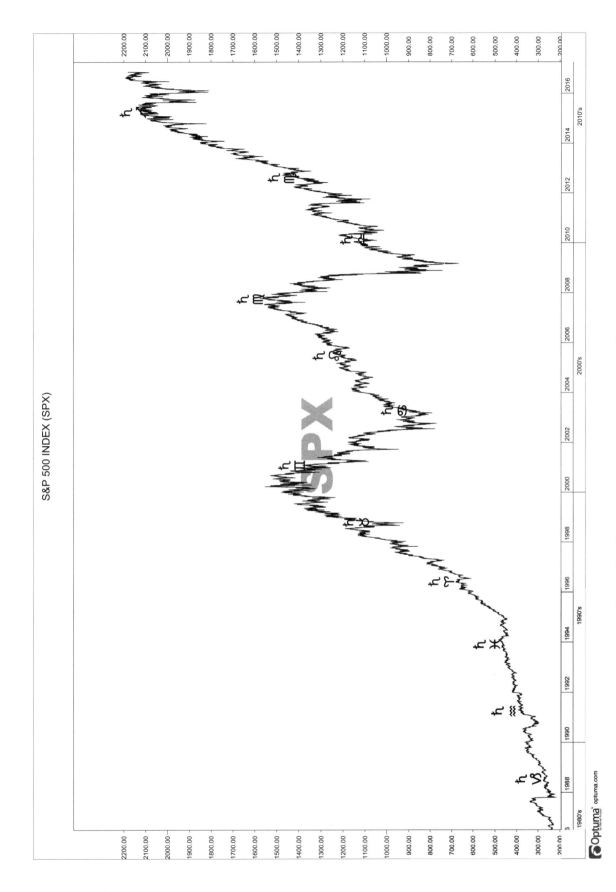

(Fig. 41) *SPX Saturn Geocentric Ingress 1990–2016*

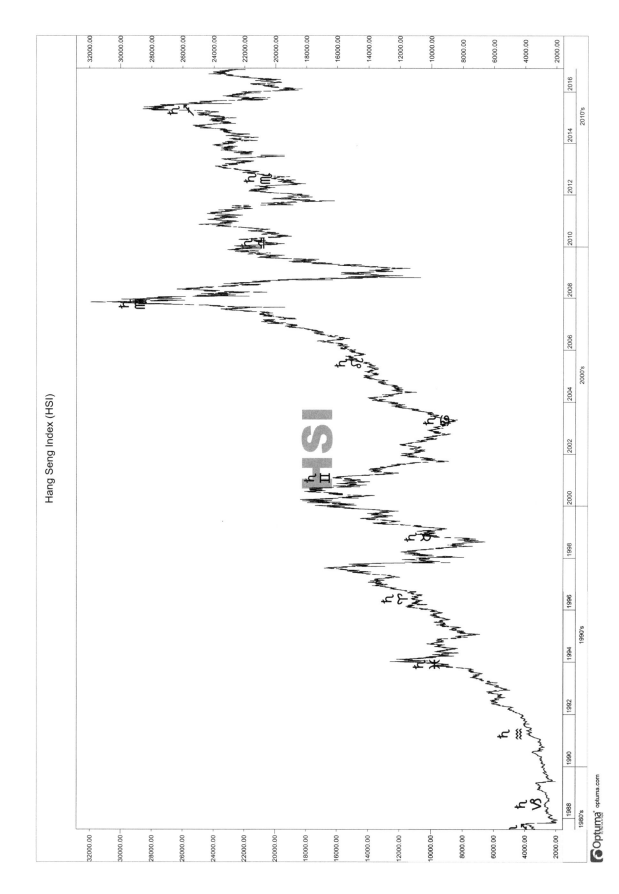

(Fig. 42) *HANG SENG Index with Saturn Geocentric Ingress 1990–2016*

through each of the Mutable signs (Gemini, Virgo, Sagittarius, and Pisces) has had decidedly negative effect. For ease of illustration the following graph, covering an almost entire Saturn cycle, uses Saturn's heliocentric ingress. Though it is true that the index is not negative for the entire duration of Saturn's transit through these signs, there is marked effect at the ingress and Saturn's transit of at least the first ten degrees of each of the Mutable signs.

These broad overviews are of interest to traders, and, in the case of Saturn, particularly so. Recall from the early chapter, "Basics," that on the three occasions when Saturn transited the degree of the Galactic center (1929, 1956, and 1987), that some traders experienced great loss. Saturn is due to make this passage again between February and May 2017.

Saturn Retrograde

Saturn's retrograde and direct stations should also be watched. These very often mark turning points. This next chart (Fig. 43)— again using the Hang Seng index—shows just how important the dates of these two stations can be. The "D" marks Saturn's direct station (when retrograde motion ceases and the point from which the planet then appears to move forward).

The relationship of the Sun to Saturn should also be noted with all aspects considered, including two aspects we have yet to consider. These are the parallel and contra-parallel aspects. The former describes the situation where both planets share the same degree of declination either North or South. A contra-parallel aspect occurs when two planets, Sun, or Moon are equidistant from the Celestial Equator, e.g. with one positioned at 5 degrees North and the other at 5 degrees South.

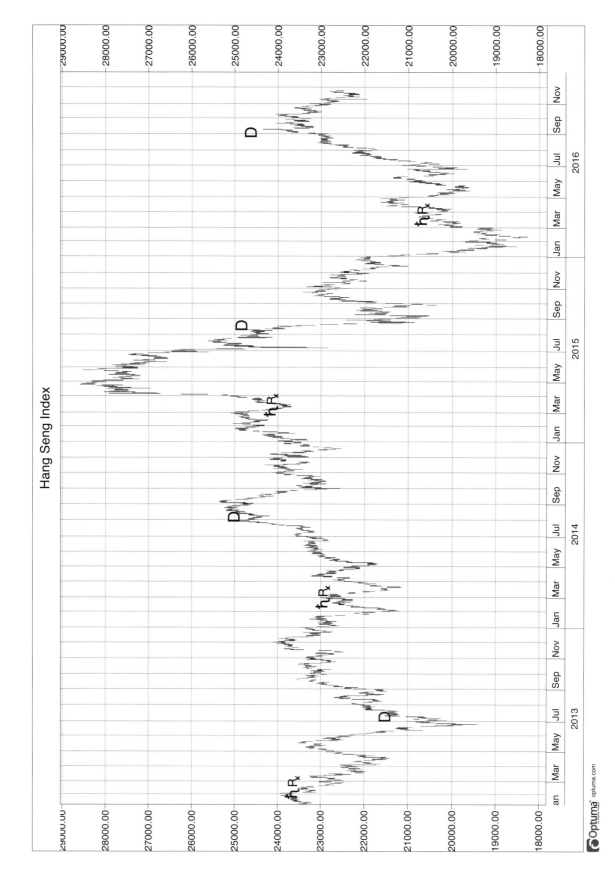

(Fig. 43) HANG SENG Index and Saturn Stations 2013–2016

This next chart (Fig. 44) considers the entire span of Saturn's transit through Scorpio and the many aspects with the Sun formed during that 30 months period. The effect of these aspects on the stock price of the StillWater Mining Company offers a useful example.

This share price of StillWater Mining Company draws special attention to the quincunx (150 degree) angle. In each instance shown, this angle has marked a minor high. We can also see that had these shares been bought at the Sun-Saturn conjunctions in either 2012 or 2013—and then sold when the aspect between the Sun and Saturn was 60 degrees—that significant profit would have been made. It may be tempting to deduce that this is a fool-proof strategy, especially when research shows that this strategy would have worked through 2009, 2010, and 2011. Yet in earlier years, it only worked 50% of the time—proving once again that one simple "astro-code" on its own is insufficient.

The Mercury-Saturn Cycle and Corn Prices

Planetary cycles can—and should—be compared to many different markets with the various commodities responding to different cycles. As the chart below shows (Fig. 45), corn does appear to respond to major aspects between Mercury and Saturn (the conjunction 0°, square 90°, and opposition 180°) as viewed heliocentrically.

Stillwater Mining Co (SWC)

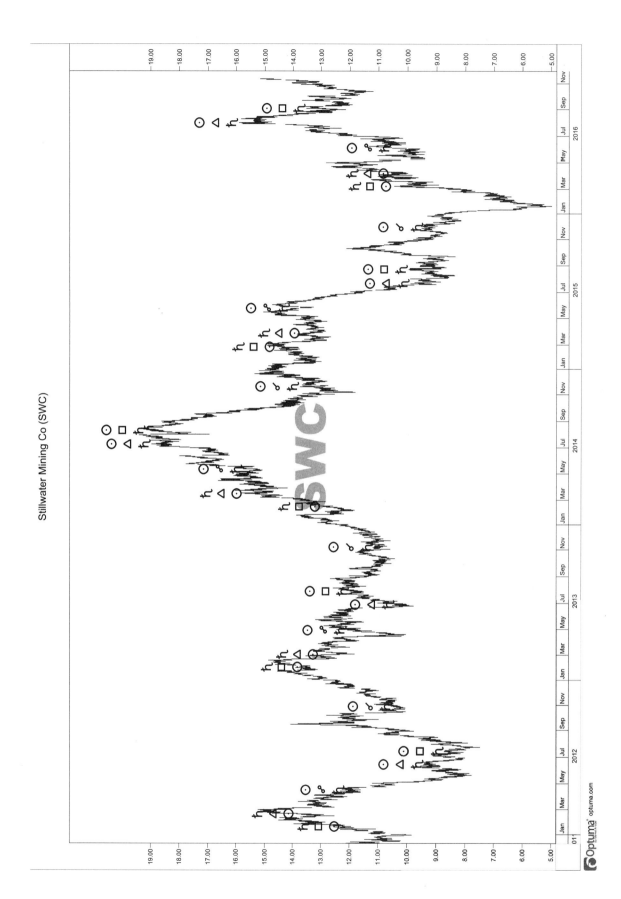

(Fig. 44) *Stillwater Mining 2012–2016 Sun Saturn Major Geocentric Aspects*

Corn (CSpot)

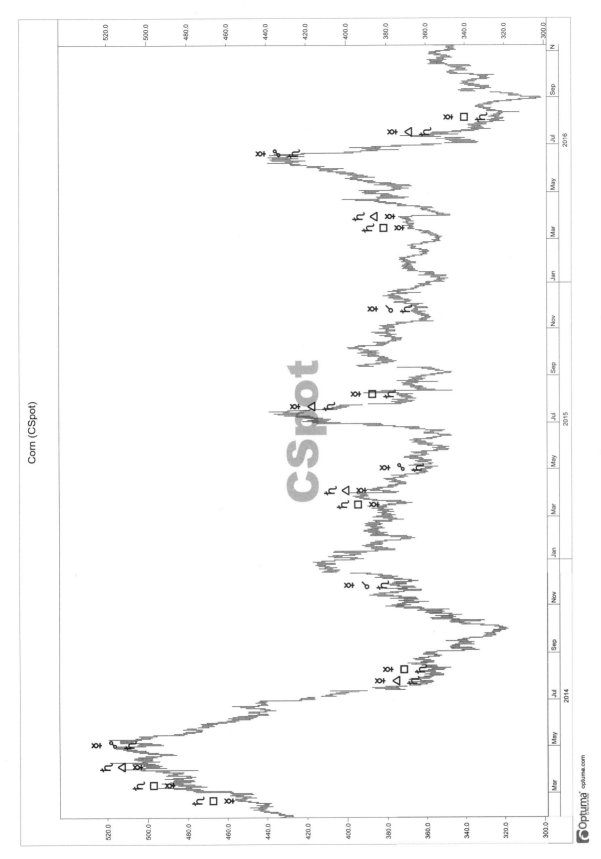

(Fig. 45) *Corn Spot Prices with Mercury–Saturn Heliocentric Aspects*

Chapter 10

Trading and the Jupiter-Saturn Cycles

A SIGNIFICANT PERIOD USED IN FINANCIAL ASTROLOGY is the approximately 20-year Jupiter-Saturn cycle. As we have seen, Jupiter is associated with expansion and, at times, with exaggeration and excess: it is after all, the largest planet in our solar system by far. If you rolled all the other known planets together, they would still not be as large as Jupiter, which spins on its axis for about eight Earth hours. It is a place of storms and thunderbolts.

In astrological terms, Jupiter has a track record of bringing more. Someone experiencing a Jupiter transit will have high expectations. If Jupiter makes favorable aspects in the chart of the CEO of a company, you can be sure that the CEO will speak optimistically and that shares will rise as a result.

By contrast, Saturn is the planet of contraction and, occasionally, of pessimism. This is one of the planets surrounded by rings. It looks as though it is contained. Saturn demands boundaries, control, and responsibility. The effect of a Saturn aspect or ingress on a share price is often to depress it—and, at the very least, marks a boundary beyond which the share price cannot go until the aspect separates, or several days from the ingress have passed.

Approximately every 20 years, Jupiter and Saturn form a longitudinal conjunction where they share a zodiacal degree. Their last conjunction was in May 2000, the previous in 1981, the one before that in 1960, and before that in 1940. Not only is there a near 20-year sequence to these dates, but there is also another pattern. Over the space of roughly a quarter of a millennium, these conjunctions all take place in one element: either Fire,

Earth, Air or Water. After approximately 12 conjunctions, the series moves from one element to another. Since the mid-18th century, each conjunction has been in an Earth sign—wherein, on a financial level, there has been focus on tangibles. In each series (Fire, Earth, Air, or Water), the penultimate conjunction heralds the coming change to the new element with a conjunction in that new element. Thus the conjunction in 1981 was in the Air sign of Libra.

We are now at the cusp of a new series where each successive conjunction will also be in an Air sign. The conjunction of 1981 offered a foretaste of the conjunctions of the 21st century. It's very interesting to note that it was during the 1980s that many of the so-called weapons of financial mass destruction were conceived. It seems likely that from the next conjunction in 2020, complex financial derivatives—and new digitalized currencies—will again develop.

As might be expected, when these two planets align, there is competition between rampant optimism and constraint. Those in business will recognize this as a moment when there is opportunity to expand but that to do so would compromise smooth running. This is where the skills of those excelling in risk assessment find their talent to be in demand. Finding the balance between risk and cautious development requires confidence—and experience.

Clearly, since Jupiter-Saturn conjunctions only occur every 20 years, this does not at first appear to be of much practical use to the trader. It would be an error of judgement to dismiss this information however. The major phases of this cycle so often determine the background "mood of the market."

Jupiter, the faster moving of the pair, will complete 2 ½ circuits of the zodiac before it re-aligns with Saturn. From conjunction to conjunction, many aspects form. Tempting as it may be to think that if indices move upward from the conjunction, then they will move downward from the opposition; study does not bear this out. There may be a few rocky weeks as Jupiter opposes Saturn but that is all. More significant moves are likely later in the cycle—from when the two planets are roughly 45 degrees away from their next conjunction. Many other minor aspects between the two planets should be noted as these too tend to bring a change of trend. At the very least, the aspects that are multiples of an eighth of the circle should be noted. There will be at least one of these in any year.

The accompanying graph covers over five years of the FTSE index with some major aspects marked (not "all" as this would make the chart more difficult to read). In many cases there is an upward trend into the aspect and a decline immediately in its aftermath. The strength of the decline varies considerably and is dependent on other factors. Consideration should be given to the signs in which the two planets are moving (Fig 46).

In 2020, Jupiter and Saturn will arrive at their next longitudinal conjunction. They do so in the 1st degree of Aquarius—an Air sign. There are many reasons to think that this next conjunction will prove a significant period for markets worldwide, especially since this particular conjunction coincides with the December Solstice. As was remarked on earlier in this work, the date on which the Sun moves into any one of the Cardinal signs carries a forward thrust energy that lasts until the next Equinox or Solstice. Whether this marks a significant low or a significant high, there is probability of major moves following this date.

Whatever the index, commodity, or share price under scrutiny, it seems likely that this conjunction will mark a significant turning point or price level. Certainly traders should be aware of such a major event.

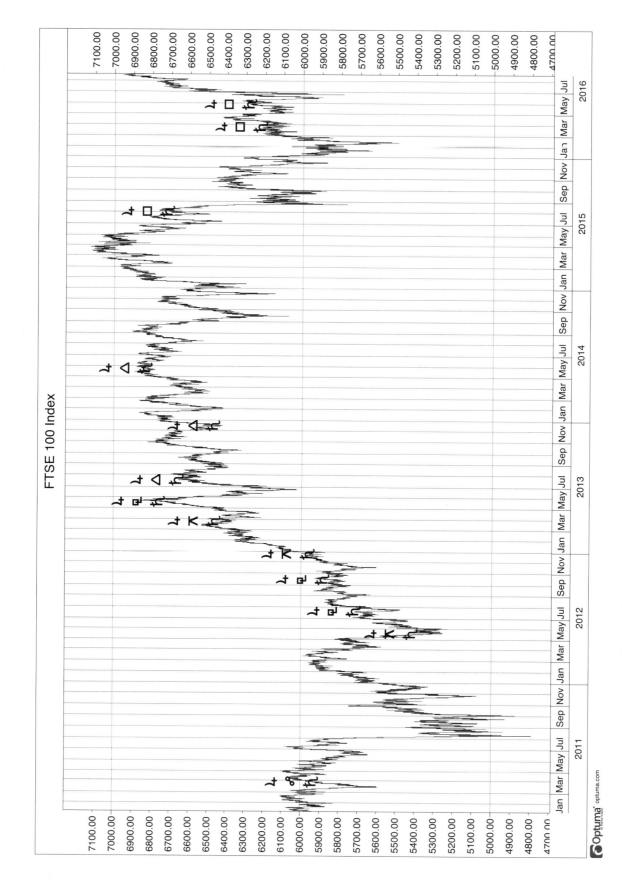

FTSE 100 Index

(Fig. 46) *FTSE Index with Major Jupiter–Saturn Geocentric Aspects*

The Declination Cycle

Consideration should also be given to the declination cycles of Jupiter and Saturn. This next graph plots the two planets as they move from North to South—the declination creating an inconstant wave in the process. Where the two lines cross, the two planets share declination. There are also occasions when the two are equidistant from the 0 degrees declination—where they are described as being in <u>contra-parallel</u>. (as explained above) *Fig 47).

Just as it is important to note the conjunctions, oppositions, and minor aspects between Jupiter and Saturn, these parallel and contra-parallel aspects should be noted by the trader. The reasons are clear when these are aspects are plotted against the Nasdaq 100 index (NDI) for 2003 (Fig. 48).

Clearly, alone, these aspects say little. Yet each marks a significant period which, when coupled with either technical analysis or other astro-features, indicates there is significance to these planetary angles.

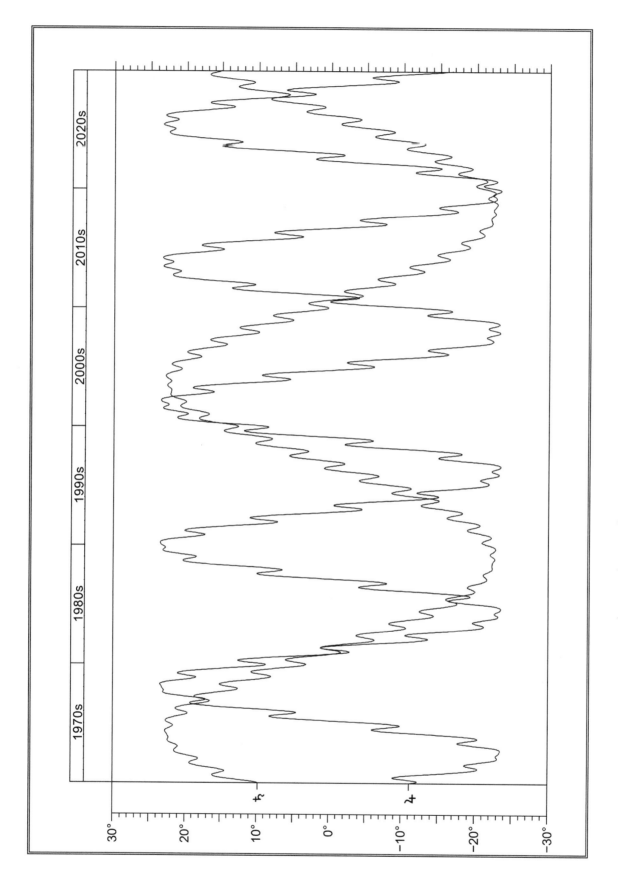

(Fig. 47) 1 Declination of Jupiter and Saturn 1970–2020

Nasdaq 100

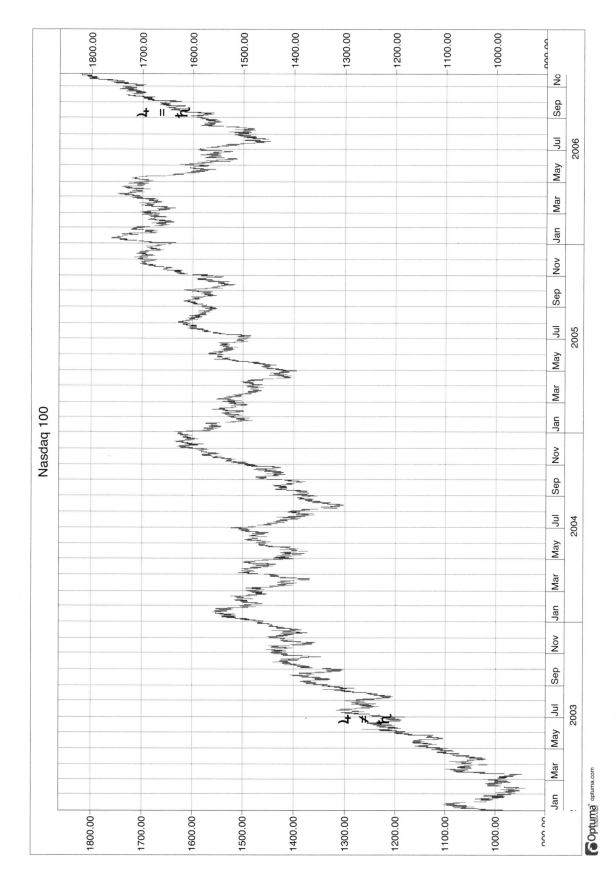

(Fig. 48) *NASDAQ 2003–2006 with Jupiter–Saturn Parallel and Contra-Parallel Aspects*

Chapter 11

Trading with Uranus

THOSE OF YOU FAMILIAR WITH THE SPAN OF PLANETARY ORBITS may be surprised to find a chapter in this book devoted to Uranus— whose 84-year orbital cycle is generally greater than the working life of most traders. Yet an understanding of Uranus' position and its interaction with other planets is most useful to consider.

Major financial panics or large scale moves have taken place as Uranus moved through the Cardinal signs of Aries, Cancer, Libra, and Capricorn. As I demonstrated in *Exploring the Financial Universe*, one highly sensitive degree area is at 19 Capricorn. Uranus last transited this degree in 2015, when considerable volatility was experienced across many markets. Actually, Uranus' transit at 19° of any of the Cardinal signs has coincided in the past with significant volatility.

Those interested in financial history will recall the story of Tulipmania. In 1637, the price of just one rare specimen fetched over 1000 guilders (the currency used in Holland in the 17th century). They will also know that when the price fell, it plummeted almost overnight and many purchasers were financially ruined as a result. These same students will also be aware of the South Sea Bubble that took place almost a century later and which again was at the root of a financial panic.

A fact of which many will be unaware is that these events were separated by an exact Uranus cycle with, in both cases, Uranus travelling through Libra: one of the Cardinal signs.

Between the South Sea Bubble and the present, almost 300 years have passed. Uranus has made four orbits of the Sun since then and as it has wended its way through the four Cardinal signs, volatility, if not outright panic, has been visible. In recent years Uranus has been making its passage through Aries—as it did in the early 1930s, when there was significant decline in major indices.

The half-way points between significant and Uranus-related falls can also be shown to bring surprises. Although Uranus' orbit is roughly 84 years, the half-way point does not take place at exactly 42 years. As with all the planets, Uranus' orbit is an ellipse, resulting in its appearing to speed through some signs and move more slowly through others. Uranus travelled through Libra (180 degrees from Aries) between 1968 and 1974: a period during which spikes in the price of oil coincided with major moves in indices. Two notable "highs" occurred in January 1973 and later in October of that same year. Uranus was then crossing 22–23 degrees of Libra. It won't return to this area of the zodiac for another eight decades.

Yet, if it is true that this degree area has resonance for the oil price, we should expect turning points in many indices (highs or lows) when Uranus is in aspect to these degrees. (The price of oil has a major effect on many industries and, thus, the share values of listed companies). An obvious place to start would be at 22–23 Capricorn in January, August, and November of 1994, which were indeed dates of some significance. March and September of 2005 when Uranus had travelled 135 degrees from 22–23 Capricorn were also significant periods.

As always, this information alone is insufficient on which to base a trading strategy. But it does provide useful background "noise" as it draws attention to a likely period of activity.

Saturn-Uranus Cycle

This cycle is long—approximately 45 years—yet is one of the major astro-economic cycles. Aspects between these two planets can be shown to correlate with sudden and sharp shocks in the market place.

This next graph (Fig. 49) is of the DJI over a two-year period during which the two planets reached 150 and 135 degree phases. It shows clear correlation with market activity.

It is common for the astro-trader to review the year as a whole, putting emphasis on aspects made by the planetary cycles involving Jupiter, Saturn, Uranus, Neptune, and Pluto. The pairing of any two of these planets warrants close study.

In considering 2015, the astro-trader, ignoring for a moment Neptune and Pluto (which we have yet to study) would mark the dates of major aspects between Jupiter and Saturn, Jupiter and Uranus, and Saturn and Uranus. As this next graph (Fig. 50) of the SPX illustrates, the effort would have been worthwhile as each of these dates proved significant.

Not all indices have a long history. The Dow Jones Index has been in existence longer than a Uranus' orbit of the Sun. It is thus possible to observe the effect on this index as Uranus moves from one sign to another (Fig. 51).

It should be noted that during Uranus' transit of Aries in the late 1920s/early 1930s there was volatility—just as is being experienced in present times. However, the movement of Uranus through Taurus in the 1930s brought some calm following the turbulence of the 1929 Wall Street Crash and the subsequent Great Depression.

It is interesting to look more closely at Uranus' transit through Aries and Taurus early in the 20th century. A knowledge of the volatility—or otherwise—of this period may be of some

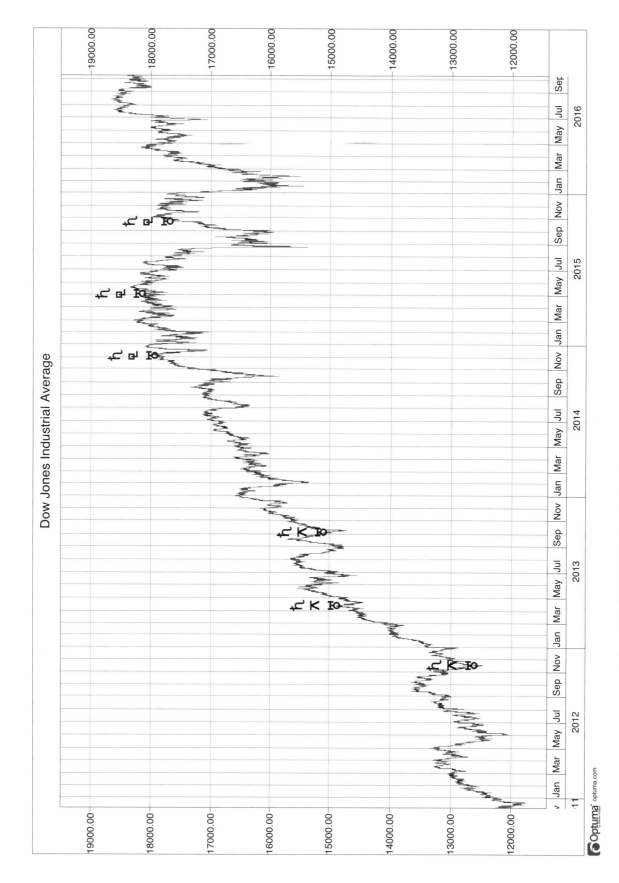

(Fig. 49) *DJI 2012-2016 with Saturn-Uranus Major Aspects Geocentric*

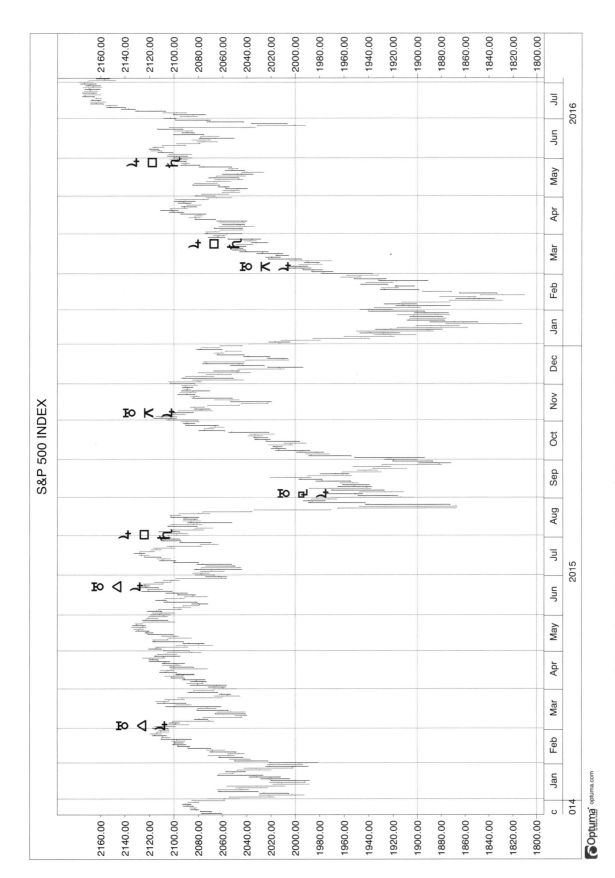

(Fig. 50) *SPX 2015–2016 with Major Jupiter–Uranus Geocentric Aspects*

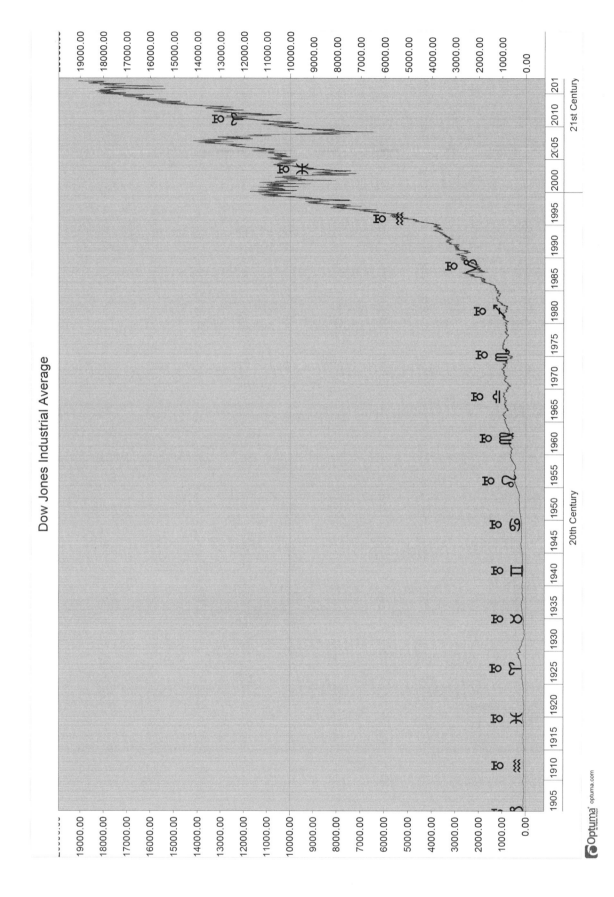

(Fig. 51) *DJI 1905-2016 with Uranus Ingress Heliocentric*

assistance in forecasting the coming years as the planet once again transits Taurus. To make this next chart even *more* interesting, the heliocentric ingresses of Mars into Aries and Libra are shown (Fig. 52).

From the heliocentric perspective, Uranus made Taurus ingress in late 1934—neatly coinciding with Mars' arrival in Aries. As we saw in the chapter on Mars, major phases in the Mars-Uranus cycle often coincide with important moments in the marketplace. It appears that the two planets changing signs together is also important. Note that the DJI gained almost 100% in the space of a year. The turning point came when the two planets opposed one another in 1937.

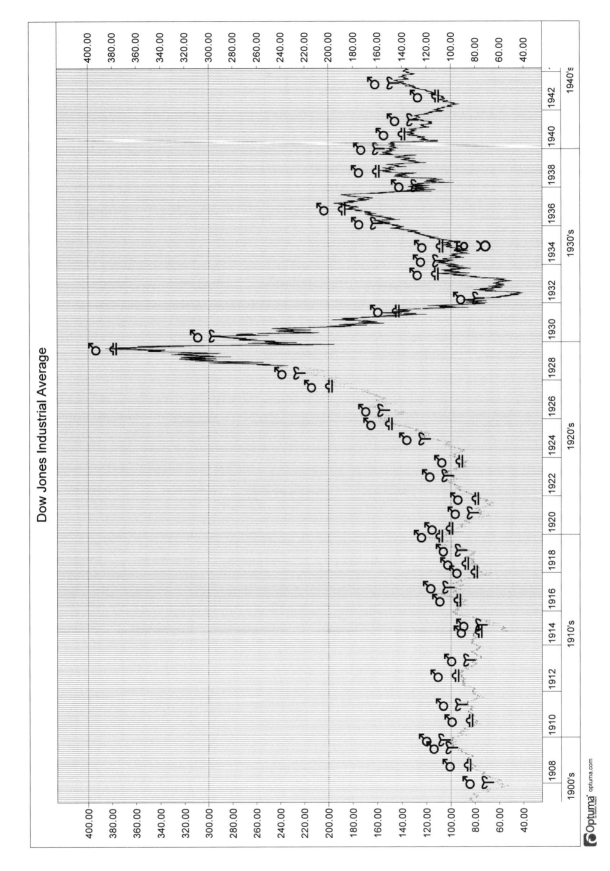

Dow Jones Industrial Average

(Fig. 52) DJI 1907–1941 with Mars Aries and Libra Ingress and Uranus Taurus Ingress

Chapter 12

Trading with Neptune

THERE IS AN ACKNOWLEDGED ASSOCIATION between Neptune and the sign of Pisces since both are strongly connected to the sea, to oil, and to the pharmaceutical industry.

The price of oil has fallen substantially since the highs in excess of $140 that were reached before the global financial crisis. As Uranus moved through Pisces (2003 to 2010), those trading in oil enjoyed a wild ride. Throughout this same period, Neptune moved through Aquarius—the sign in which Uranus is said to operate best. During those years, then, Uranus and Neptune, each moving through a sign preferred by the other, were in what astrologers call "mutual reception." This relationship added to the high probability of a turbulent period in both Uranus- and Neptune-related industries.

Mutual reception ended as Uranus moved from Pisces to Aries (2010) and Neptune from Aquarius to Pisces (2011). Collapse in oil prices can be traced to Neptune's ingress into Pisces. Note that the last "high" did not coincide with either the heliocentric or geocentric ingress but within weeks of those events.

There are many methods for trading oil. This next example looks at Light, Sweet Crude Futures. Other "oil" charts produce similar results.

When Neptune reached 0 Pisces, it was 330 degrees from the start of the zodiac (0 Aries). Allowing $0.10 per degree, the Neptune line will correlate to a price level of $33 (shown as a dark horizontal line near the foot of this graph) (Fig. 53). Increments of 15 degrees are then drawn. As Neptune is never stationary, and using geocentric positions, the Neptune line is not exactly

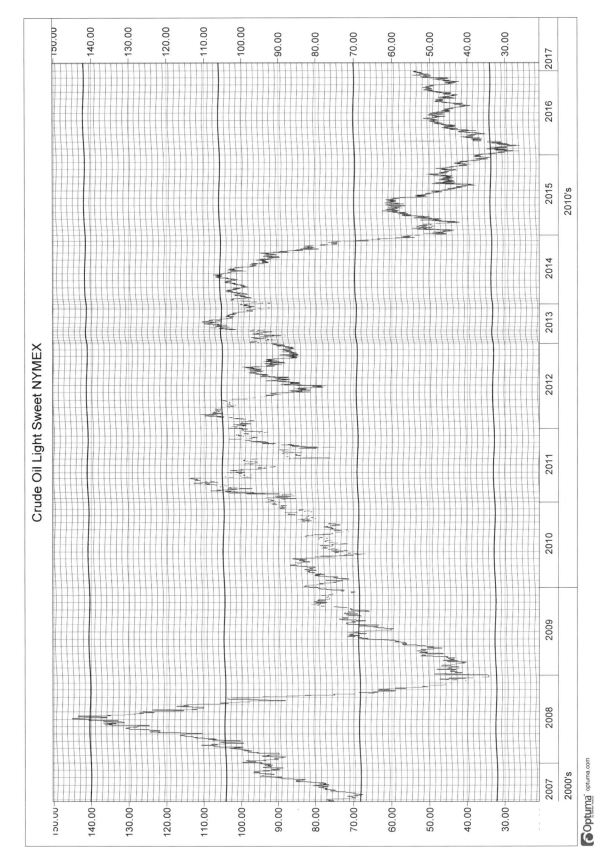

(Fig. 53) *Light Sweet Crude Oil 2008-2016 Neptune Line*

straight, appearing to undulate: rising and falling (as Neptune turns retrograde).

The results are striking and show clear price levels. Note that the 2008 low was almost exactly the Neptune line but that the low of 2016 dipped below, which can be explained by another factor (covered at the end of this chapter) .

As with the study of any index, commodity, or share price, many factors must be taken into account.

The co-ruler of Pisces is Jupiter so that aspects made between Jupiter and Neptune should also be taken into consideration.

Superimposed on this next chart (Fig. 54) for Light, Sweet Crude Oil Futures are geocentric aspects including parallels and contra-parallels between Jupiter and Neptune. A different time frame is used in this example in order to focus upon the many aspects that happened during the period between the conjunction of these two planets in 2009 and their opposition in 2015. Though this chart still does not tell the full story, the results are more than a little interesting as several major turning points coincide with aspects between these two planets. Note particularly that minor highs have coincided with the two planets being 30, 60, or 120 degrees apart.

Those trading in oil would surely wish to know more about the major lows in January 2009 and July 2016. Both lows have in common a Sun-Jupiter conjunction, but in different signs: Aquarius and Virgo. (It is not the case that every Sun-Jupiter conjunction brings a low though it does appear that this aspect and the opposition coincide with turning points).

A book could be written about the history of the price of oil and its correlation with planetary cycles. For the present, this next graph, again of Oil Futures, marks basic aspects in the heliocentric Mars-Neptune cycle (conjunction, squares, and

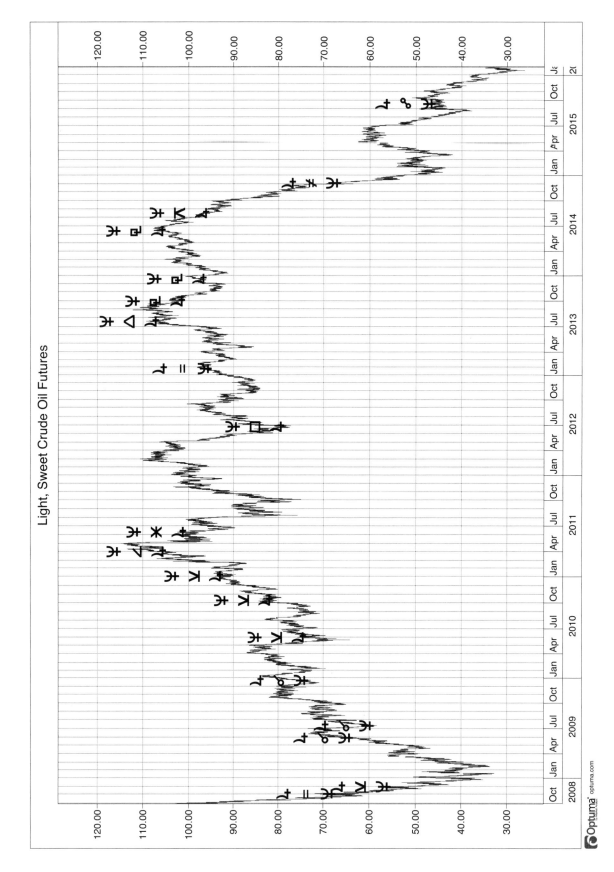

(Fig. 54) *Light Sweet Crude Oil with Jupiter–Neptune Aspects Geocentric*

opposition). These aspects very often mark clear turning points as well. As always, both geocentric and heliocentric positions should be taken into consideration. To be clear: though these aspects will likely occur on different dates, both have relevance. Ignoring one perspective is unwise. Change in trend can occur at the exact geocentric aspect or the heliocentric aspect. When combined with technical analysis, a decision as to which is the most likely to mark change of trend can be made.

Note that until Neptune leaves Pisces in 2025, these aspects will always occur in the same signs: the conjunction in Pisces, the first square in Mutable Gemini, the opposition in Virgo, and the final square in Sagittarius (Fig. 55).

To return though to the lows of January 2016: These coincided with aspects between Venus and Neptune. Neptune was, as explained, moving through Pisces. In January, Venus was in Sagittarius forming a quintile (72° or a fifth of a circle) aspect to Neptune, and, at the other low in February, was 45 degrees (eighth of a circle) from Neptune (Fig. 56).

Clearly there are many factors to take into account when trading oil futures. What *should* be clear from the notes above is that aspects to Neptune are best noted. In the case of the last example, the fact that the two key aspects took place close to Venus' ingresses indicated the probability of change of direction.

Johnson and Johnson

This next chart (Fig. 57) is rich with information. Covering the period since the global financial crash in 2008 and through to the September 2016 Equinox, each retrograde station of Jupiter and Neptune is marked. These stations often mark turning points. Both Jupiter and Neptune have just one retrograde period every

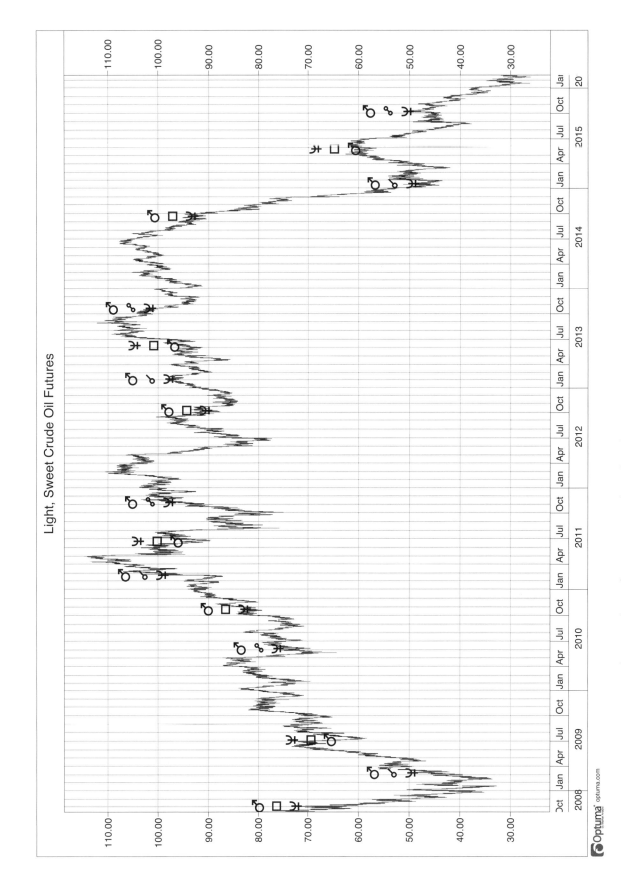

(Fig. 55) *Light Sweet Crude Oil with Mars Neptune Aspects Geocentric*

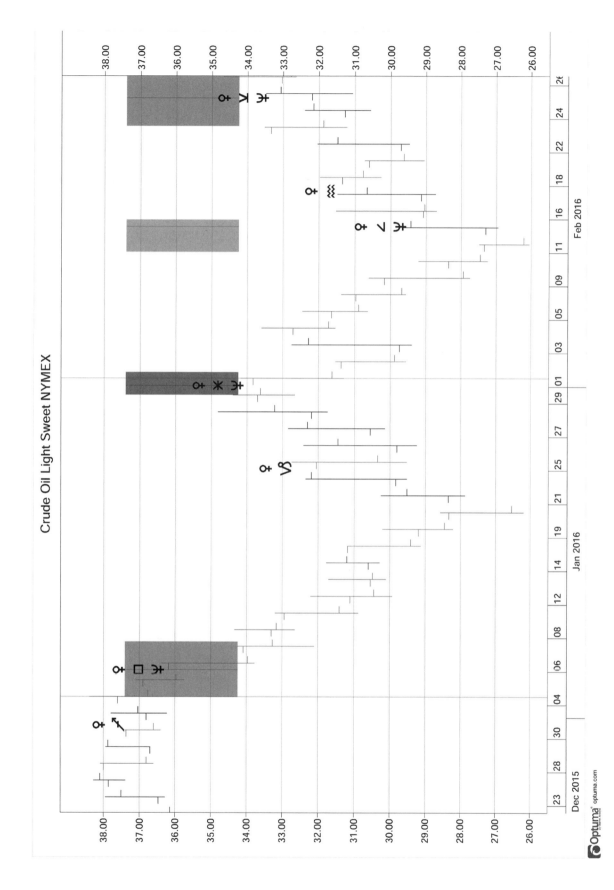

Crude Oil Light Sweet NYMEX

(Fig. 56) *Crude Oil NYMEX 2015–2016 Venus Ingress and Venus Neptune Aspects Geocentric*

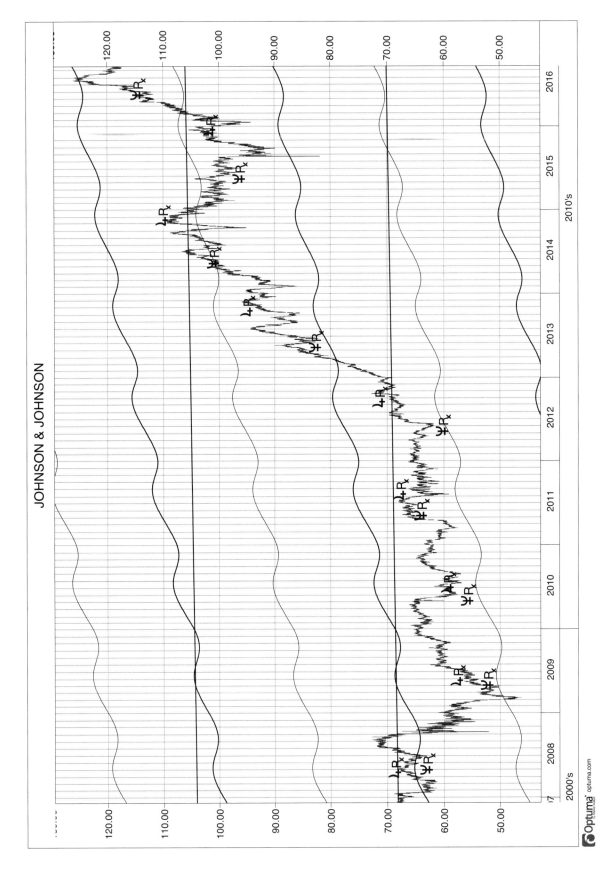

JOHNSON & JOHNSON

(Fig. 57) *Johnson & Johnson 2008–2016 Jupiter and Neptune Lines with Retrograde Stations* year. In the case of Jupiter, the retrograde station suggests a top, at which point the investor might wish to take profits.

Next, we observe the Neptune lines which appear almost horizontal. Their intersection with the waved line formed by Jupiter marks sensitive price levels. At the time of writing the price is falling. Attention then falls to $108 (Neptune line) and $110 (Jupiter line). The price is likely to fall to at least this level.

Chapter 13

Trading with Pluto

PLUTO IS NOT THE "PLANET OF DOOM" although it often receives bad press from some astrologers. A slow-mover—it takes the better part of a quarter of a century to travel through all 12 signs of the zodiac—Pluto plays a key role in financial astrology. Those years when the planet moves from one sign to another (which varies since it can spend as short a time as eight years in one sign and as long as 20 years in another) usually prove dramatic when it comes to financial markets. The most recent ingress was in 2008 when Pluto's arrival in Capricorn coincided with the near-collapse of the global financial markets.

As was fully documented by examples in my book *Exploring the Financial Universe*, the greatest financial events of the 20th century each showed Pluto to be at an important angle with other planets as financial panics and dramas took place. In particular, its passage over 19° of any of the Cardinal signs (in the 20th century that included 19 degrees of Cancer and 19 degrees of Libra), brought singular events and challenges to the fore. At the time of writing this book, Pluto has yet to complete its transit over 19° of Capricorn. If past patterns repeat, it seems likely that dramatic events will take place in 2017.

Pluto's passage over any single degree takes at least several weeks—if not some months—given the annual periods when it is retrograde. Pluto appears to stand still twice in any year. These stations should be marked in trading diaries as—when they coincide with other major aspects or ingress—there is increased probability of dramatic development.

An excellent example of this principle in action occurred in

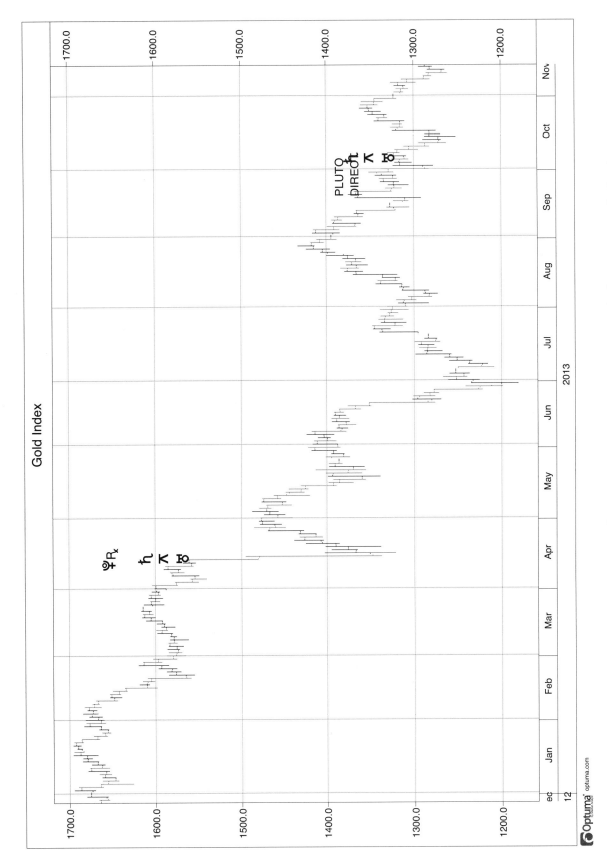

(Fig. 58) *Gold Index 2013 with Saturn–Uranus Major Aspect and Pluto Retrograde Station*

April 2013 when Pluto's retrograde station coincided with Saturn and Uranus forming a 150° angle to each other. Pluto turned retrograde on the Friday as that aspect became exact. The price of gold moved five percent that day. Over the course of the weekend, other factors came into play and the price moved a further few percent on the Monday (Fig. 58).

One of the key words used for Pluto is manipulation. Whatever prompted the sharp moves, they were not entirely unexpected. Financial astrologers felt that mining stocks would be affected.

Of course, it is not always the case that a Pluto station coincides with either a major aspect between two slow-moving planets, lunations, or an ingress. Yet since Pluto only stations twice a year, it is not an onerous task to check to see if these stations will coincide with such an event.

Pluto-Jupiter

All cycles have import, but the Jupiter-Pluto cycle should be given particular attention. It is sometimes called the "wealth cycle." Its duration is around 12 years, and, as with all cycles, has phases similar to those of the Sun-Moon. This next chart looks at the interaction of these phases on the SPX (Fig. 59).

What is striking in the above chart is that the SPX often rises in the days leading into a Jupiter-Pluto aspect and then loses momentum when it is passed. Of special interest here is the turning point reached after many of the quincunxes (150 degree aspects). On most occasions, the index has lost momentum directly after this aspect and declined in the following days.

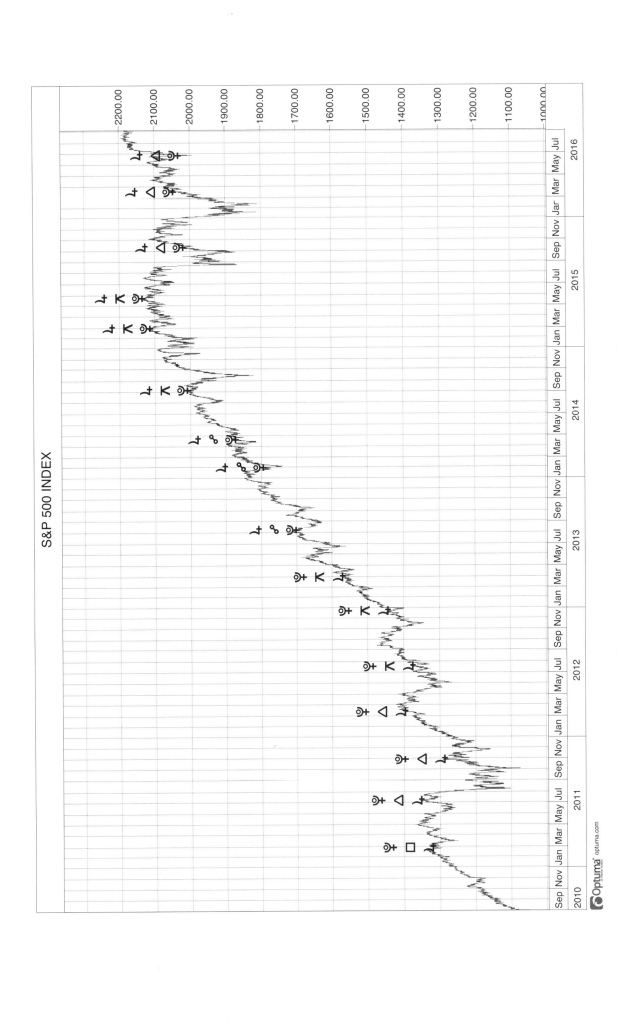

S&P 500 INDEX

(Fig. 59) SPX 2011–2016 Jupiter–Pluto Major Aspects Geocentric

Pluto-Sun

Pluto, as "God of the Underworld" is often associated with precious metals. A study of Sun-Pluto aspects and the Silver index suggests a possible link. This study looks only at Sun-Pluto aspects since Pluto arrived in Capricorn in 2008. Every Sun-Pluto conjunction since 2008 has been in Capricorn, with every opposition taking place when the Sun is moving through Cancer.

Note the length of the bars on dates around the Sun-Pluto opposition in the next chart. These indicate particular volatility and could now be anticipated every year. True, these moves do not occur on the exact date of the opposition. But, knowing the high probability of large moves around this time, and having taken into consideration other factors—while making full use of technical analysis—it should be possible to arrive at a suitable trading strategy.

The two trine aspects take place with the Sun situated in either Taurus or Virgo. This makes for an interesting study. The Sun, in the tropical zodiac system used in this work, can never be retrograde. But Pluto can. Presently, and owing to Pluto's eccentric orbit, Sun-Pluto conjunctions are taking place while Pluto is far away from the Sun and never when Pluto is retrograde. The two trines and the opposition each take place when Pluto is retrograde. The square aspects between the Sun and Pluto occur with Pluto in direct motion.

It cannot be said often enough that many factors need to be taken into consideration. Yet evidence suggests that immediately following a Sun-Pluto square or opposition, the Silver index is most likely to decline.

The dates of the 120 degree (trine) aspects should also be noted. It is not uncommon for these to mark a minor top. At the very least they seem to mark price levels of interest (Fig. 60).

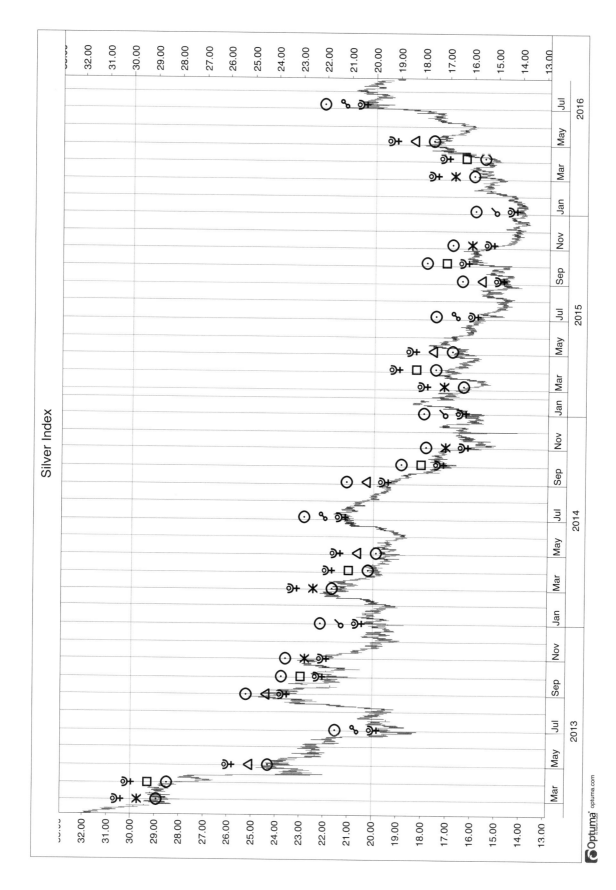

(Fig. 60) *Silver Index Sun-Pluto Major Aspects*

Saturn-Pluto

If Jupiter-Pluto constitutes an overt "wealth cycle," then the Saturn-Pluto cycle could be considered the "stealth-wealth" cycle. Those born with these two planets at critical phase in their cycle (conjunct, square, or in opposition) can be shown to build wealth slowly and steadily. Bill Gates of Microsoft is an excellent example. This is also true of countries that came into being at one of these phases (e.g. Saudi Arabia).

The Saturn-Pluto cycle varies between 32 and 37 years in length. The first major phase, from conjunction to opposition, tends to be one of controlled and sustained growth. That rhythm can be broken at the opposition, when banks or governments place restrictions and rein in the money supply. The latter part of the cycle is treacherous as a result, with capital denied to those who could prosper given the opportunity. Such opportunity often comes at the conjunction when rules are relaxed and encouragement given to investors.

The most recent conjunction was in 1982. The decade that followed certainly witnessed expansion (the Yuppie era). It came to a halt at the opposition in 2001/2002. The next conjunction is in 2020.

Though a relatively long-term cycle, Saturn's relationship to Pluto offers useful background information to traders and to long-term investors. The latter may choose the conjunction as an optimum time to invest. As this next cycle begins within 18 months of a low in the nodal cycle, 2020 could yet provide excellent investment opportunity.

Chapter 14

Trading with Eclipses and Lunar Nodes

THE SUN'S APPARENT PATH against the backdrop of the stars is called the Ecliptic. The Moon too makes a path. These paths intersect twice: with one known as the Moon's North Node and the other as the Moon's South Node. These points in space (they are simple intersections) appear to travel backwards through the zodiac: thus instead of moving from 0 degrees Aries through each successive sign, they move backwards through Pisces, then Aquarius and so on._ The entire nodal cycle occurs over a 19-year period, similar in duration to the Jupiter-Saturn cycle, another "business" cycle found to have particular relevance for the financial astrologer.

At least twice in any year—and occasionally as many as five times—the Lunar Nodes are within a few degrees of a New Moon resulting in a Solar Eclipse. It is possible too that at the Full Moon—either two weeks before or after the Solar Eclipse—the Nodes will be close enough to the degrees involved for a Lunar Eclipse to take place.

It is absolutely NOT the case that markets will always react to either a solar or lunar eclipse and dramatically change direction. Yet these celestial events are important. Often there is marked reaction when the Sun is 90 or 180 degrees (square or opposition) from the most recent solar eclipse. It can also be shown that when a planet reaches the degree of a recent eclipse it acts as a trigger and then there is marked reaction.

The big question must be: "How can you tell if an eclipse is important or not?" It is reasonable to assume that a lunar eclipse will bring enhanced Full Moon reaction—increased volume of trade if not actual volatility.

A solar eclipse is quite different: it is a special type of New Moon that only occurs when the Sun and Moon are aligned within a few degrees of one of the Moon's nodes. As stated, a solar eclipse does not always bring marked reaction, yet often marks a change of market mood.

This next graph (Fig. 61) covers three years of SPX trading. Note that a lunar eclipse can occur on either side of a solar eclipse and occasionally on both. Note too that steep drop and rebound between the solar and lunar eclipse in 2014.

Could that immediate fall after the lunar eclipse have been forecast? The answer is yes, and that it was. That lunar eclipse chart showed Uranus aligned with the Full Moon. The Sun was moving through Libra, and the Moon and Uranus were in Aries. Uranus is the planet associated with shocks and surprises and, on cue, markets overreacted—only to recover by the solar eclipse two weeks later.

We might reasonably deduce that for markets to respond immediately to a solar or lunar eclipse, either must be part of a celestial configuration involving another planet. This information is not difficult to find. The date and time of eclipses is given in many diaries and there are a number of astrology programs available as apps so that the chart can easily be created. If there is a planet positioned either with or at right angles to the eclipse, then there is greater likelihood of strong market move.

What to make, though, of those eclipses where it appears "nothing has happened"? As suggested above, reaction is most likely when the degree of the eclipse is triggered by another planet passing over this degree. Financial astrologers often make

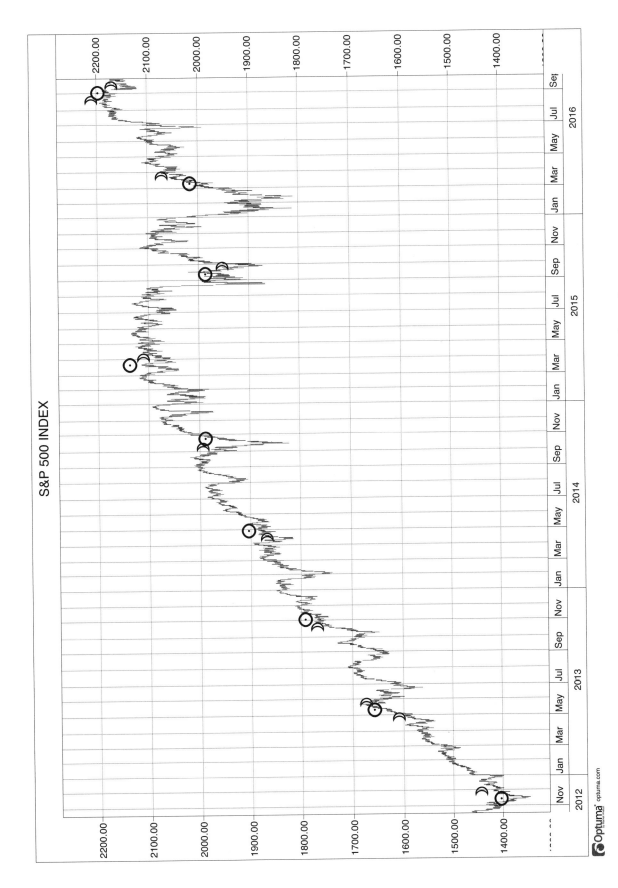

(Fig. 61) *SPX 2012–2016 with Lunar and Solar Eclipses*

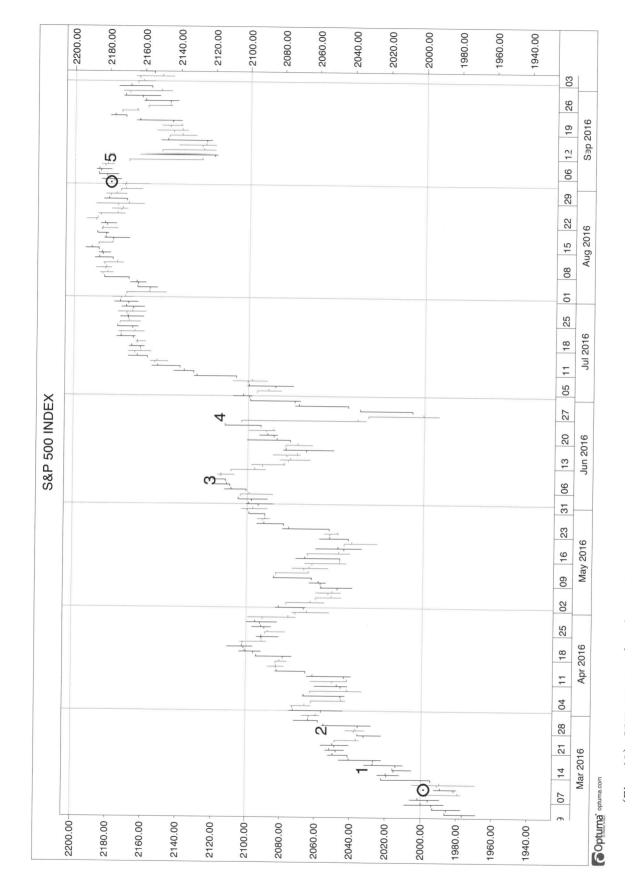

(Fig. 62) *SPX 2016 with Solar Eclipse and Marking Dates when the Eclipse Degree Is Affected by Planet Transits*

note of eclipse degrees and the dates when these are crossed by other planets.

Example

The chart opposite (Fig. 62) shows market activity following a solar eclipse and various planetary aspects over a six-month period. The solar eclipse on March 9, 2016 was at 18° Pisces. Mercury arrived at 18 Pisces on March 15 (1), and Venus on March 27 (2). Venus crossed 18 Gemini (90 degrees from Pisces) on June 8 (3), and Mercury made similar aspect on June 24 (4), while Mars was 90 degrees from this "hot" degree on September 9 (5). This last date marked Jupiter's Libra ingress. Each of these dates would be marked as likely to see sharp movement. Note particularly the strength of movement on the dates 90 degrees from the eclipse (points 3, 4, and 5). The probability of above average movement increases if, on the selected date, there is another key indicator (major aspect or ingress).

In the 1930s, Louise McWhirter established a cycle via her research. She determined that as the North Lunar Node travels "backward" through the six zodiac signs between Aquarius and Leo (recall that the Lunar Nodes are usually moving in reverse order to the norm),[1] business volume in the United States grows. With that growth comes increase in price. Furthermore, what is now known as the McWhirter Business Cycle suggests that once the Node has completed its passage through Leo and moved into Cancer, there will be distinct decline in volume and value. Business sentiment between the North Lunar Node transit of

---

1 See discussion of mean and True positions on page 159. In the accompanying graphs, the mean node is shown with a hyphen above the glyph.

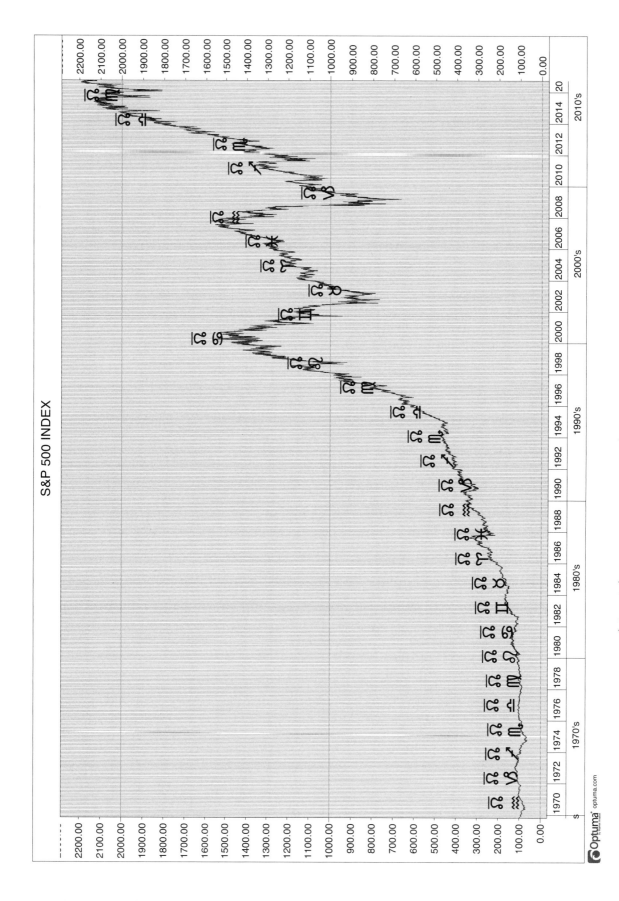

(Fig. 63) SPX 1970–2016 with Mean Lunar Node by Sign

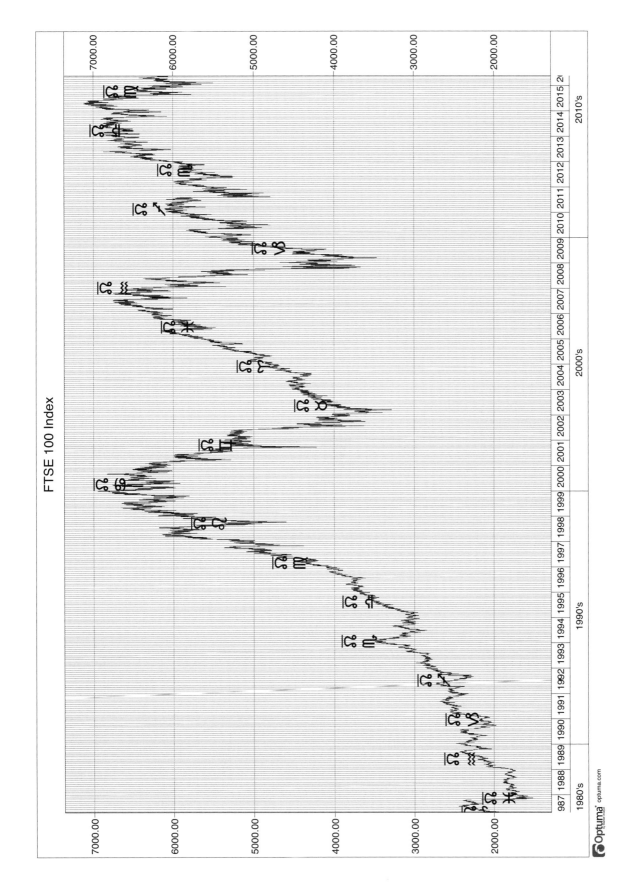

FTSE 100 Index

(Fig. 64) *FTSE 1980–2016 with Mean Lunar Node by Sign*

ALL ORDINARIES

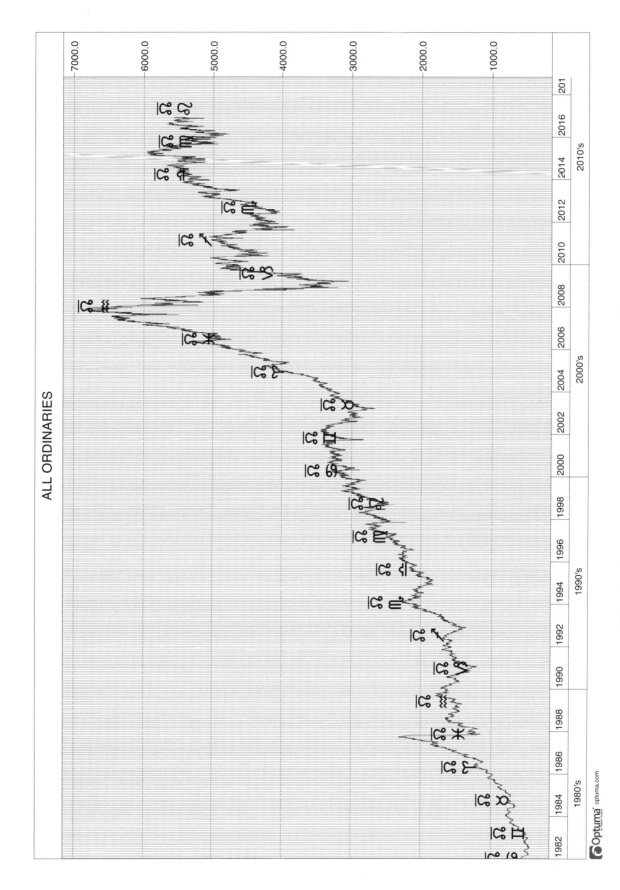

(Fig. 65) *ALL ORDS 1980-2016 with Mean Node by Sign*

Cancer until it arrives back in Aquarius indicates a consistent downward trend.

This rhythm has held true—at least in the United States whose markets appear highly sensitive to the Lunar Node cycle. As can be seen in the next three graphs, other markets react differently (Figs. 63 [SPX], 64 FTSE, and 65 [ALL ORDS]).

There is variation between the various indices (given above are the SPX, FTSE, and XAO). But there is also reasonable consistency in that all three saw major decline as the Node arrived in either Cancer or Aquarius.

Using this rule, we would determine that significant decline in these indices would next occur when the Node moves into Cancer in November 2018. Note, though, that this shift might not be an immediate one. In the instances above, it may be seen that the Node will move some way through that sign before decline begins.

This "sign information" offers useful background information to the trader and to long term investors. The latter may well choose to wait until a significant low is reached—perhaps even a few years until, perhaps, the Node is making a Taurus passage—before once again investing.

What is of far greater interest to the frequent trader is the interaction of the Lunar Node with the planets. As the nodal cycle travels through the zodiac it forms conjunctions, squares, and oppositions with each. Where interaction is with, for example, Mercury, any effect tends to be short-lived. With slower moving planets involved, then a trend may dominate for several weeks.

In 2016, both the Lunar Node and Jupiter moved through Virgo. Though the two were very close to conjunction at the start of the year, they did not reach mathematical exactitude until June

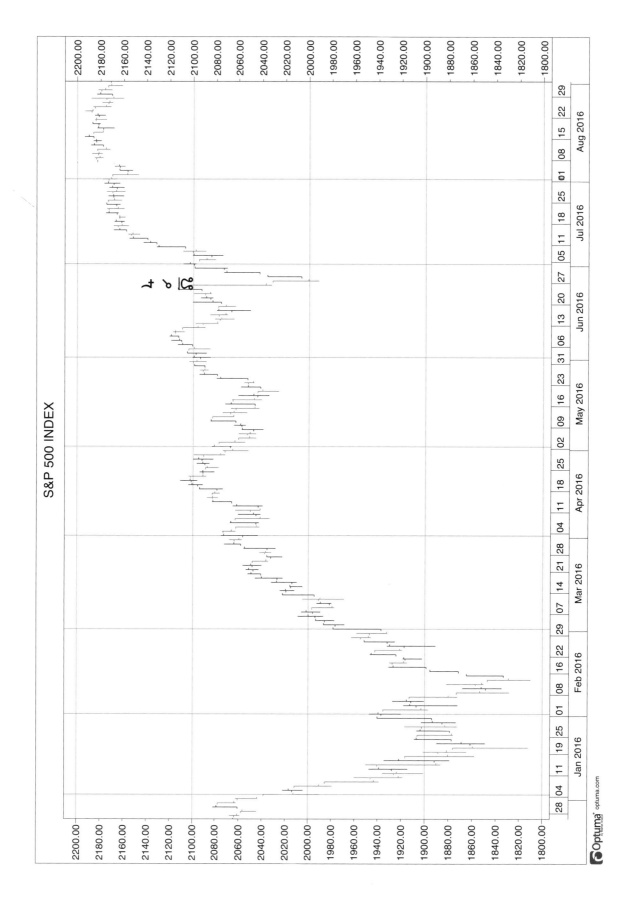

S&P 500 INDEX

(Fig. 66) SPX 2016 with Jupiter Conjunct Lunar North Node

24th—the day after the Brexit vote. The next graph shows the SPX for that period (Fig. 66).

Though interesting, there is still insufficient information on which to trade. Unusually, Mercury was travelling through Virgo during the summer months of 2016, eventually forming a conjunction with the Node in that sign. Note that Mercury's various alignments with the Node often signal significant activity—though this is still insufficient information on which to trade (Fig. 67).

This next graph (Fig. 68), again of the SPX, marks conjunctions between the lunar north node and the outer planets. Each has marked a minor top.

MEAN OR TRUE NODE:

As a result of variations in the gravitational pull between Earth and Moon, there is a 'wobble' effect or oscillation effect on the position of the Lunar Nodes. The True Node takes account of this oscillation whereas the Mean Node takes the average. The True Node can at times appear stationary or to be in forward motion whereas the Mean Node always appears retrograde.)

(Fig. 67) SPX 2015-2016 with Mercury-Node Aspects

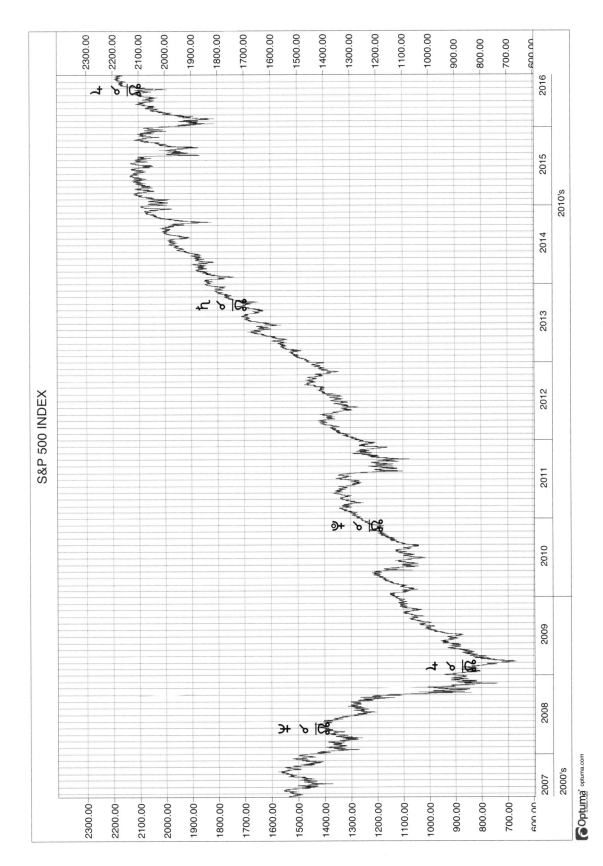

(Fig. 68) *SPX 2007-2016 with Lunar Node Outer Planet Conjunctions*

Chapter 15

Trading Using Angles and Day Charts

THE TERM 'HOROSCOPE' MEANS, QUITE SIMPLY, a "map of the hour" with each of these cosmic signature having unique features depending on exactly where you are in the world and the exact time of day for the start of an event.

With markets opening at different times and in different places across the world, they have different starting—and finishing—times. Both are important: with some financial astrologers calculating these times weeks in advance and identifying which days are likely to see significant activity.

It is common to consider the "start" of a chart as being the Ascendant or rising degree. This is calculated for both the start and the finish of, for example, the Wall Street trading day. The Descendant (its opposite) is 180° from the Ascendant and is also an important point or angle.

Another axis of the horoscope must be taken into account. This axis also divides the chart into two halves giving two more angles. At one end of the axis is the MC or Midheaven. At the other end, 180 degrees from it, is the IC or Immum Coeli. During the course of the day this axis moves: the Midheaven ticking over at a set rate of approximately 1° every four minutes. Thus, during each hour of trading on Wall Street the Midheaven will travel a full 15°. As the hours pass, it is probable that there will be certain times when the Midheaven is exactly aligned with the Sun, Moon, a planet, or other celestial body.

By contrast with the Midheaven, the number of degrees covered by the Ascendant in the course of each trading hour is dependent on the actual place and time of year.

It is not at all unusual for the financial astrologer to calculate the charts for both the opening and closing bell on Wall Street or open and close for another market. At different times of the year, it is entirely possible that one of these angles will be shared by the position of the Moon or one of the planets. The Sun, of course, can only be aligned with the Ascendant if the specified market opens exactly at dawn. There is no time during the year when dawn occurs at 9:30 a.m. (opening bell) in New York. In start of trading day charts in New York, the Sun will always be above the horizon in the upper hemisphere of the chart. At some point during the trading day, the Sun will align with the Midheaven, usually somewhere between midday and 1 o'clock. During winter months, the Sun may be very close to the Descendant at close of trade.

The situation with the Moon is quite different. During the course of the trading year, there are times when the Moon does indeed align with either the Ascendant, or the Descendant, or the other two angles. On these dates, we would anticipate that volume would be above normal. This is because the Moon is associated with moodiness and, often, mass reaction or movement.

There are occasions when the Moon appears close to one of these angles alongside another planet.[1] For the unwitting astrologer, this presents something of a pitfall. As the declination is not shown on the usual horoscope dial, they may think the angle aligns with the Moon and the planet at the same time—only to find that there is a difference caused by a difference in declination. Regular astrology programs do not always show this, however, it is possible to find software that will list both.

---

1   Of course, in reality, that planet will be thousands and thousands of miles away from the Moon. They might not even be in pure and exact alignment. That can only happen when the two share the same degree of the zodiac and are at the same declination: a rare event indeed.

(Fig. 69) Table of the Moon and the Trading Day			
Example / Day / Event List			
TIME	ASC	MC	EVENT
12.41	0° Gemini	27° Capricorn	
12.51	3° Gemini	0° Aquarius	
12.53	4° Gemini		Square Node
12.59	6° Gemini		Square Venus
13.08	9° Gemini		Conjunct Moon
13.31	16° Gemini		Square Mars
13.45			Moon Rises
13.54	22° Gemini		Opposes Saturn

A printout may offer listing, as shown above. (Fig. 69):

Key information here includes those moments when the Ascendant or Midheaven change signs, or the Sun, Moon, or planet arrives at key positions. This is of little interest to anyone other than day traders. To these people though, knowing the exact moment when there is likely to be a cosmic energy shift can be invaluable. Currency traders in particular have been known to use this information to their advantage.

Day Charts

Knowing which aspects will become exact during the course of the trading day is also useful. Preparing a list is a worthwhile exercise and is one of my weekend tasks.

Though it is of some interest to cast a chart for the time that a market opens, I tend to focus on the chart for close of trade. Note that not all markets close at the same time of day: most close on the hour, a few on the half-hour. A Close of Trade chart for the

All Ordinaries in Sydney is unusual in that an extra 12 minutes is allowed to tidy up transactions. Charts for this index would be drawn for 16.12 local time.

It is very often the case that when a market closes with a planet EXACT on one of the angles of the chart for the precise location, then that day's trading is notable—sometimes strikingly so.

Though general planetary patterns affect all markets, it is quite possible for the market in Wall Street to close with a very different lunar aspect to the one in Sydney (there being a near 12-hour difference). A day that closes with an exact Moon-Uranus opposition in Sydney has produced shock results and strong moves that are not experienced in other parts of the world.

Observations on Annual Close of Trade Charts and Longer Term Trends

Of particular interest are the Close of Trade charts at the end of each year. It is common in January for the various investment houses to give their opinion on where indices will be as the year closes. In my work I take into account long-term planet cycles, the position of the Nodes and the close of trade charts for each index at the end of the year.

Throughout 2015, the Nodal Axis was in an up-curve of the McWhirter Business Cycle—indicating growth.[2] Of the major cycles, Uranus and Pluto were due to form a major aspect in March, signaling possible upset, while in November, Saturn and Neptune would form the first of a series of right-angles, indicating dampening prospects. On these factors alone, I concluded that indices would end the year lower.

Arriving at the probable closing figure required review of the

---

2   See page 116.

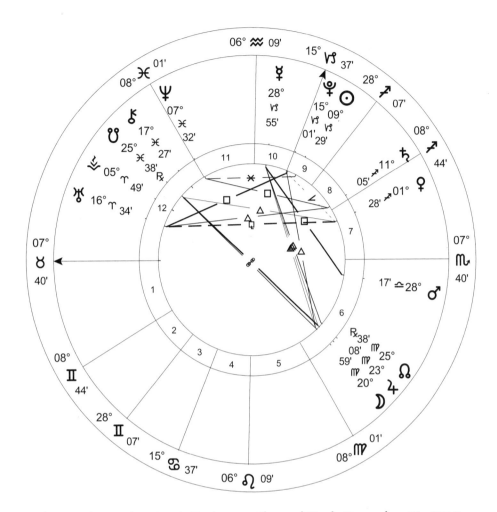

(Fig. 70) *London Stock Exchange Close of Trade December 31, 2015.*

end of year trading chart (Fig. 70). The London Stock Exchange closed for the year at 12.30 pm on New Year's Eve (December 31st).

As may be seen, Pluto was exactly aligned with the Midheaven: indicating a powerful conclusion to trading for the year. This is, of course, the close of trade chart for both the day and the year. That being the case, greatest emphasis is given to the position of the slow moving planets and their aspects. In this instance, with Saturn having recently formed a right-angle to Neptune, there was high probability that 2015 would see significant losses—at least where UK markets were concerned. In fact, the FTSE closed five percent down on the year.

The same exercise for Wall Street delivered rather different results (Fig. 71):

Here Neptune is exact at the Midheaven suggesting a confused picture. This chart also showed the Moon exactly aligned with the Lunar North Node (an "up" signal). Results in the US were indeed very different than those in the United Kingdom. The Dow Jones index closed down less than one percent on the year while the NASDAQ composite ended the year in positive territory.

What should be obvious from this example is that although study of end of trade charts is interesting, it does not offer an unambiguous result.

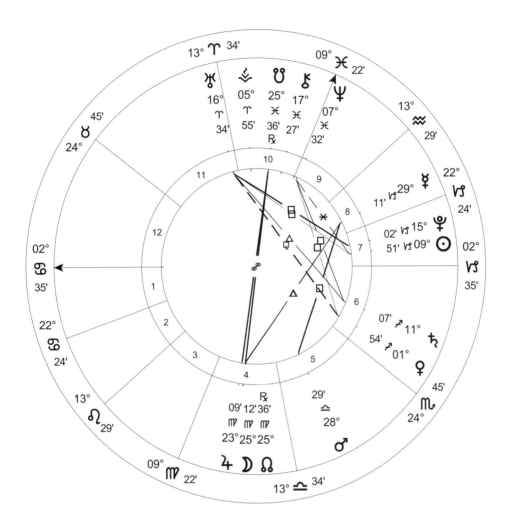

(Fig. 71) *Wall Street Close of Trade December 31, 2015.*

Chapter 16

In Closing

It should now be obvious that no single solar, lunar, or planetary-based factor is sufficient to devise a trading strategy. Please note, too, that this book is a Beginner's Guide. There has not, as yet, been mention of the role of asteroids and Transneptunian planets, the Fixed stars, or even the arrival of comets. Yet it should also be clear that the addition of astro-based studies to a financial trading toolbox will not only be useful, but has the potential to offer a trading edge.

The important question is what to do next? It would be all too easy to be overwhelmed by possibilities. As with mastery of anything, a bite-sized and structured approach works well. You can, of course, throw yourself in at the deep end, but would then most likely end up "learning the hard way."

Clearly there is need for some tools and reference points. The main essential is an ephemeris. These are available in either digital or book format. Whatever the format of these ephemerides, these are books of tables that plot the positions of the planets, the Sun, and Moon. They are usually based on either noon or midnight. Ephemeris tables also give the dates of every ingress, or entrance of a planet into a sign, together with latitude and longitudinal positions. There are heliocentric and geocentric ephemerides. My experience has been that traders make most use of the pocket-sized version produced each year by Foulshams under the title of *Raphael's Ephemeris*. This is a less than $10 investment.

There are also, many, many apps and software programs available.

The technical charts used throughout this work have been built using the astro platform within the Optuma program with which I am most familiar. There are other software programs: FAR and Timing Solutions to name but two.

In this final section of the book, my aim is not to sell you on any particular product, but rather to guide you through the early steps of using your newfound knowledge.

Putting It All Together:

It sounds obvious: but first you must determine which markets you intend to study! You can't look at everything.

Over the years I have looked at many markets and now regret that I didn't focus. The wider you spread the net, the more likely you are to find "something that fits"—and always works the first time. The temptation then is to increase the investment next time, only to lose.

To incorporate astro-cycles into your trading toolbox, you need to become a master detective or code breaker. What works with one trading platform may not work with another.

In your early practice, I would suggest that you choose a single index—one commodity and one share price. Give yourself a long timeframe—6 months minimum—to determine which techniques work for you and that you are happy to put to use. There is no harm in playing "FANTASY astro-investing" and testing theories and strategies. Indeed, it could be argued that this would be the wisest investment of your time.

I urge students NOT to invest in expensive software when they first start. W. D. Gann, who was noted as an able and talented investor who made use of the cycles of the planets, did not have access to these. Rather, he worked with raw data, graph paper, and an ephemeris.

By noting daily price movement and comparing this with planetary movement, you can build your own arsenal of knowledge—remembering always that what works in one area may not work as well in another. Once you get to know to which planetary cycles your stock, index, commodity, or currency pairing responds, there is the potential to make gain.

That said, even with this information you will need market experience. You might well find value in learning at least the basics of technical analysis. There is no need to prepare to fail by being unprepared. There is no short-cut to private study.

Many examples in this work used the SPX. It is a popular index and many cycles can be plotted against it. Whichever index you choose, you might like to make a note of dates when there is increased volume or above-average moves, and the close-of-trade charts for those days. This dossier of charts will prove invaluable for later study.

For commodities it is imperative that you use one source of information. Prices on one exchange can differ from others. Some prefer to use the London Metal Exchange, others the Chicago Exchange.

Where shares are concerned, it is wise to choose a company with long history. Back-testing is essential, and the longer the period of time with which you have to work, the better. In the Intermediate Book we will be following a share price using both Incorporation and First Trade charts. These can work exceptionally well. Valuable information though can be gleaned without the data that these charts require. Learning to work without a "starting date chart" is important—as uncovering incorporation and first trade charts is not always easy, particularly in certain countries where the information is hard to come by.

Here then is my recommended procedure.

Background information: review the year as a whole.

How I wish I had carried out this exercise when I first began. Understanding general trends is imperative.

Note sunspot activity and whether the trend is toward solar maximum or minimum. (Minima is expected in 2019.)

Does the nodal cycle suggest that the business cycle is on the way up or down?

Will any of the slower planets change signs during the year? When? Note the date geocentrically and heliocentrically

List major aspects in the slow-moving cycles (for example: Saturn opposing Uranus, or Jupiter conjunct Saturn). Pay attention to the declination cycle. Having identified these major aspects, check to see if they coincide with any of the major lunar phases: eclipse, New Moon, Full Moon, apogee or perigee, maximum North or South declination or latitude. Is the collective picture indicative of business confidence or the opposite?

Will either Venus or Mars turn retrograde in the year? Make note of the dates. If these are in the past, then make note of index or price levels at these events.

Geocentric Mercury will be retrograde three times during the year. Make note of the dates and zodiacal degrees. Make a historical check of similar retrogrades and note the effect on the areas in which you are interested.

Ascertain the amount of change (if any) as the Sun moves from one sign to another.

Any of the astro-trading programs will mark the Sun's move from one sign to the next.

As shown in our chapter on the Sun, there is a seasonal effect with the indices. Check if a similar effect is observable with the market behavior of your particular interest. In this, consider a minimum of 20 years. You may find that, for example, for 10 years, a share price rises consistently as the Sun moves into Taurus only to lose value at this ingress in the next ten-year period.

Note in particular if there is any striking movement as the Sun moves into one of the Cardinal signs of Aries, Cancer, Libra or Capricorn. Later, you may wish to test the half-way points between these signs—as when the Sun crosses 15 degrees of each of the Fixed signs of Taurus, Leo, Scorpio, and Aquarius.

Moon phases

Observe if there is increase or decline (need not be steady), between one lunar phase and another. You might consider New to First Quarter, or Full, or Last Quarter Moon, or any mix of these.

As shown in the lunar chapter, maximum declination varies over the course of a decade. In the case of commodities—especially silver—note those years when lunar declination exceeded 23 degrees and 26 minutes and is therefore "out of bounds." Did this affect your chosen share, index, or commodity?

Are there major moves at apogee or perigee?

Does the Moon's move from North to South latitude (i.e., 0 latitude) or the Moon's maximum North or South latitude position correlate with a high or low in the market under investigation?

Does your share, commodity or index respond to a particular planetary ingress?

Start with Mars—and check both heliocentric and geocentric ingresses. If there are promising indicators, make a note of forthcoming ingresses and mark these in your trading diary.

Mars retrograde tends to affect whole markets. Check to see if your particular chosen stock, commodity, or index is affected more than the whole index or sector.

What happened when Mars was at maximum declination?

Carry out the Mars' exercises for Venus too.

Plot Sun-Mercury conjunctions and Mercury retrograde periods against your technical charts. As before, it may be that the whole market moved at a Mercury station or Sun-Mercury conjunction. Did your chart move more than the average for the sector or index? If there were sharp moves at a Mercury station, note the degree of that station and, where possible, check to see what happened when Mercury stationed near to this position in earlier years (you will need several years' worth of data for this exercise)

Next, take a recent high and low.

What were the dates?

How many days between them? Does this link to a planet's orbit or length of a cycle with another planet? Did either the high or low coincide with an ingress? If it did, what happened in previous years at similar points of ingress?

Determine the positions of the planets at close of trade on those dates. Don't forget their declination and latitude positions.

With the above list of positions, consider first the major aspects at the high and the low. For example: perhaps the high coincided with Mars 120 degrees (trine) from Jupiter, and the low with the two planets 15 degrees apart. Check then to see if there is a tendency for aspects between these two planets to bring a day or two of volatility.

If there is no apparent correlation aspect-wise, then check to see, for example, how far Mars had travelled. If it had travelled 135 degrees, then see what happened 135 degrees prior to the high. Was that also a low?

Yes, there is much to test and to back test and this is just the start! Among the many areas yet to explore are planetary lines, planet speed, asteroids, the influence of Jupiter's Moons, and more. All these will be covered in our forthcoming Intermediate Guide.

If, while waiting for that work, you are inspired to learn more, the list of Internet sites in Appendix 3 will provide a series of rich resource.

Appendix 1

Stock Exchange Birth Data

New York Stock Exchange (NYSE) : May 17, 1792, Wall Street, New York. No exact time available. Jack Gillen gives 8:52 am as Local time, and Louise McWhirter gives 7:52 am as Local time.

Dow Jones Index : July 3, 1884, 10:00 am New York.

Japanese Stock Market (NIKKEI) : May 16, 1949 – no time known. (use 9:00 am Local time).

Johannesburg Stock Exchange : November 8, 1887 – no time known, try 9:00 am local time).

London Stock Exchange (FTSE) : Founded in 1801. (Chart in common use is cast for January 3, 1984 at 9:00 am.)

Hang Seng Index : November 24, 1969. In the absence of accurate "start" time, 9:00 am local time is used.

NASDAQ : February 8, 1971 10:00 am New York.

FEDERAL RESERVE : December 23, 1913. 6:00 pm EST Washington.

Appendix 2

Chart of the October 1987 Market Crash

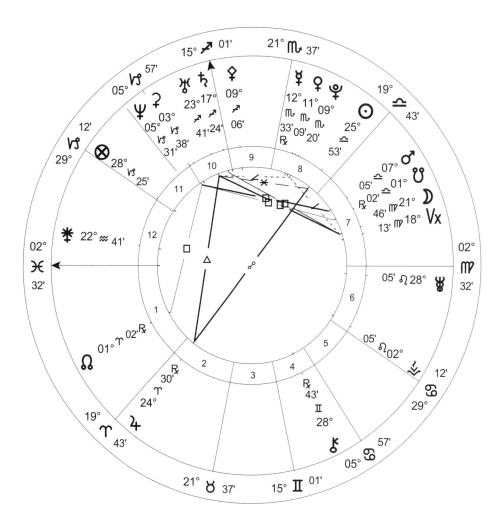

(Fig. 72) *October 19, 1987, 16.00 BST London.*

Glossary of Terms

APOGEE: The point in an orbit when the Moon, planet or satellite is furthest away from Earth

ASPECTS: Apparent angles between planets or sensitive points of a horoscope.

ALIGNMENTS: Generally used to describe conjunctions when two stellar bodies (Sun, Moon, Asteroids or Planets) appear in a straight line as viewed from either the Sun or Earth

ASC: Short for Ascendant (rising degree) and describing the degree of the zodiac on the Eastern horizon for an exact time at precise location.

CARDINAL: Term used to describe the signs Aries, Cancer, Libra or Capricorn. Respectively these begin at the March Equinox, Summer Solstice, Autumn Equinox and Winter Solstice

CELESTIAL EQUATOR: The projection of the Earth's Equator into space

CONJUNCTION: When the Moon and another orbiting body in the solar system share the same degree.

CONSTELLATIONS: Groupings of stars.

CONTRA-PARALLEL: An aspect in declination when two planets share the same degree of declination, but one is North and the other is South of the celestial equator.

CULMINATING DEGREE: Usually refers to the arrival of a planet or the Moon at the Midheaven

DECLINATION: The angular distance of a planet North or South of the Celestial Equator

DIRECT STATION: The zodiacal degree from which a planet appears to move forward after a retrograde period.

ECLIPTIC: The apparent path of the Sun on the celestial sphere.

EPHEMERIDES: Tables used in astronomy, astrology and celestial navigation giving the daily positions of the planets and Moon.

GALACTIC CENTER: The apparent source of the gravitational forces in a galaxy

GLYPHS: Symbols used to represent planets or signs

HARMONICS: Are based on the principles of resonance. They are the mathematical arrangements of the planets and sensitive points. It is useful to think of these as 'aspects under the microscope'.

HOROSCOPE: from the Greek, meaning 'map of the hour'. Generally describing a circle containing the positions of Sun, Moon, planets ad some asteroids.

INGRESS: The term used to describe the entry of a planet or Moon into a new sign.

NODE: Usually refers to the Moon (though all planets have nodes). This is where the Moon (or a planet) crosses the ecliptic moving north by declination. The south node, in the case of the Moon, is in exact opposition and marks that point in space where the Moon crosses the ecliptic moving south.

MEAN and TRUE NODE: The Moon's orbital plane is not stable and appears to have a wobble. The Moon's Nodes appear to travel backwards at a rate of approximately 3 minutes of arc each day. This is not consistent thanks to the wobble effect. There are times when the lunar node is in forward motion. The true node uses the actual position whereas the Mean node is the average and is always retrograde.

MILKY WAY: The galaxy within which our solar system is contained

MUTABLE: The signs Gemini, Virgo, Sagittarius and Pisces are each termed Mutable implying obvious levels of versatility and flexibility.

NODAL CYCLE: For the Moon's node to travel from 0 Aries through the signs of the zodiac back to 0 Aries is a period of approximately 18.6 years

OPPOSITION: The term used to describe an aspect or angle of 180 degrees between two planets or sensitive points.

OUT OF BOUNDS: A planet is considered **out-of-bounds** when it travels beyond the ecliptic, or beyond 23°27' in north or south declination

PARALLEL: Term for an aspect in declination when two planets share the same degree of declination, with both either in North or South declination.

PERIGEE: Closest to Earth

PLANETARY CYCLES: The period between a set starting point: usually between two planets: from one conjunction to the next.

RETROGRADE: Describes the situation where, relative to Earth, a planet appears to travel backwards.

RISING DEGREE: Also referred to as the Ascendant, describing the degree of the zodiac on the horizon at an exact time and location.

SENSITIVE POINTS: Usually includes the Ascendant and its opposite, the Descendant, the Midheaven (MC) and its opposite, the IC.

SOLAR APEX: The point on the celestial sphere, near the star Vega, toward which the solar system is moving relative to the visible stars

SQUARE: Term for an aspect describing when two planets or sensitive points are at 90 degrees apart.

TECHNICAL ANALYSIS: A trading tool evaluating securities in an attempt to forecast their future movement by analyzing statistics gathered from historical prices and volume.

TRANSITS: the relationship between the Sun, Moon or planets at a given period of time (usually the present) to a fixed even

TRANSNEPTUNIAN: Hypothetical planets

TRINE: Term for an aspect describing when two planets or sensitive points are 120 degrees apart.

Bibliography

Tim Bost: www.timbost.com

Graham Bates: Author with Jane Chrzanowska Bowles of *Money and the Markets* published by Aquarius Press

Donald Bradley: www.bradleysiderograph.com

Malcolm Bucholz: www.investingsuccess.ca/

Arch Crawford: www.crawfordperspectives.com

Christopher Carolan: *The Spiral Calendar* published by New Classics Library

Edward Dewey: (1895-1978): Further information at www.cyclesresearchinstitute.org

W.D. Gann: www.wdgann.com Many works including: *Tunnel Through the Air* published by Gann

Jack Gillen: www.astrologyresearcher.com Author *The Key to Stock Market Speculation* published by AFA

Mike Harding: co-author *Mundane Astrology* by Michael Baigent, Charles Harvey and Nicholas Campion published by Aquarian

Charles Harvey: co-author *Mundane Astrology* by Michael Baigent, Charles Harvey and Nicholas Campion published by Aquarian

Alphee Lavoie: www.alphee.com

Bonnie Lee Hill: www.bonniehill.net

Mitch Lewis: www.mitchastro.com

L. J. Jensen: author *Astro-Cycles and Speculative Markets* published by Lambert-Gann Publishing

Edward Johndro: author: *The Stars: How and Where They Influence*

Theodore Landscheit: www.landscheidt.info

Robert T.H.Lee and Peter A. Tryde: *Timing Solutions for Swing Traders* by published by Wiley

Hans Lenz: offers a subscription market newsletter

Jeanne Long: www.galacticinvestor.com

Charles Matlock: author: *Man and Cosmos*

Ray Merriman: www.mmacycles.com and author *The Gold and Silver Book*

Bill Meridian: www.billmeridian.com

David McMinn: www.davidmcminn.com

Louise McWhirter: author: *Astrology and Stock Market Forecasting* published by ASI

Olga Morales: www.astrologyforganntraders.com

Grace Morris: www.astroeconomics.com

Rebecca Nolan: offers a financial newsletter

Dan Pallant: wrote for many publications including the London-based *Financial Times*

Larry Pesavento: author of *Harmonic Vibrations* published by Traders Press. website: www.larrypesavento.com

Thomas Reider: author: *Sun Spots, Stars, and the Stock Market*

Marcus Rose: www.rosecast.com

Georgia Stathis: www.starcycles.com

Henry Weingarten: www.afund.com

David Williams: author: *Financial Astrology*

Manfred Zimmel: www.amanita.at

Also, for further information:

http://time-price-research-astrofin.blogspot.com/

SOFTWARE:

www.magiastrology.com

www.astrolabe.com

www.optuma.com

www.timingsolutions.com

www.trineaspects.com

www.lunatictrader.com

Index

About the Author

CHRISTEEN H. SKINNER is the author of the best selling book from Ibis Press *Exploring the Financial Universe*, as well as *Money Signs* and *The Financial Universe*. She is a practicing astrologer based in London, with clients all over the world. She works with entrepreneurs and traders and is Director of Cityscopes London, a company specializing in future casting. She holds a Diploma from the Faculty of Astrological Studies where she taught for a decade. She has been Chair of the Astrological Association of Great Britain, Chair of the Advisory Board of National Council for Geocosmic Research, and is a Trustee of the Urania Trust and a Director of the Alexandria I-Base project. She offers a free monthly newsletter service now in its eighth year.

Exploring the Financial Universe
The Role of the Sun and Planets and Financial Activity

CHRISTEEN H. SKINNER

- A view of the correlation between planetary cycles and financial markets
- Forecasts for 2017 and beyond
- The author is well respected and active in the field of Financial Astrology

The role of the Sun, planets and stars and their influence on global markets is intriguing to traders and investors alike. Christeen Skinner's research shows very definite links between major stock market movements and the position of the planets. This book will be of interest to those with little understanding of astrology as well as to those well-versed in the subject. The work includes charts, graphs and horoscopes and explanation of some of the techniques used for astro-financial forecasting.

In *Exploring the Financial Universe*, financial astrologer Christeen Skinner covers solar rhythms and the intricacies of commodity, property and currency price movements with planet cycles. The role of the planets in mastering the relationship between time and price is considered. There is chapter on the natal horoscope and financial rhythms set from birth. The book concludes with forecasts covering 2017–2024.

Chapters include: Stock Market Crashes of the 20th century; Currencies and major planetary configurations; Commodity price movements; Property price cycles and the role of the Moon and planets; The link between planet cycles, time and price; Financial timing indicators in your own chart; Forecasts 2017–2024

The author presents case studies in business astrology and an explanation of some astro-finance trading techniques.

Illustrated with financial charts taken from the Optuma software program for astro-traders.

$22.95 • ISBN: 978-089254-218-5 • Ebook: 978-089254-632-9
Paperback • 6 x 9 • 224 pages • Illustrated